D1807749

Candle Making Secrets

By

Jennifer Furgeson

Table of Contents

Introduction
Page 3

Chapter One: History of Candles and Candle Making
Page 6

Chapter Two: Candle Making Supplies
Page 16

Chapter Three: What Every Candle Needs: Wax, Wick, Color and Scent
Page 22

Chapter Four: The Basic Steps and Troubleshooting
Page 36

Chapter Five: Making Candles
Page 48

Chapter Six: Candles As Gift Ideas
Page 67

Chapter Seven: Make a Wish and Blow Out a Candle: Making Your Business Dreams Come True
Page 72

Conclusion
Page 78

Appendix: Essential Tools of Candle Making

Page 79

References
Page 80

INTRODUCTION

They say confession is good for the soul. I'm not sure that's true, but I do have a confession to make: I am not a naturally born craft aficionado.

In fact, for most of my teen and adult life, I resisted any activity that had the word "craft" attached to it. I don't knit. I don't crochet. Let's face, I try real hard not even to cook. (Only when my back is up against the wall.)

I caved in once with the craft activity. I got talked into trying my hand at "stamping." You know what I'm talking about. Those stamp pads with the cute designs, stamp some ink on them, then create fabulous cards, letterhead and who knows what else.

The women I was with created stunning pieces of stationery. Mine looked like a first grader did it!

Why do I tell you all of this? Because I am now a "dyed in the wool" official proponent of making candles. I can't believe how beautiful my projects turn out. My candles are so nice, in fact, that I have my own creations in just about every room of my house.

Not only that, but I've been presenting them as gifts to family and friends for the last several years -- birthdays, Christmas, Easter. No matter what the holiday, I have a candle for it. Geez, sometimes I give a candle just as a "I've-been-thinking-about-you" gift.

And people really appreciate them. That bolsters my self-esteem. And in fact, I've even started to sell them to various outlets -- with more success than I thought I would have.

There's really a point to all of this explanation. Even if you don't think that you're the "crafty" person, you may discover that candles bring out the inner craftsperson in you. It certainly did in me.

Even if you've shunned -- or more appropriately failed -- at every other craft, you'll find that candle making is unlike any other craft you've ever done.

For one thing, you really don't need to have any inner type of talent. Let's face it, if I can be successful at making candles anyone can!

If you're thinking of starting this quite fascinating hobby, then by all means, do. Don't let past failures at craft projects hold you back. Don't let a lack of "craft knowledge" place any type of doubt in your mind.

Candle making is, without a doubt, the most fun you'll ever have creating anything. By the time you've completed your first candle, your wax won't be the only thing that will be melted.

Your heart will melt as well, because you'd have fallen in love with this easy activity. But you'll also love this activity because it won't send your checking account plummeting into double digit deficits.

You can easily start your hobby on items you probably already have around the house already.

How to Use This Book Wisely

Read through this book once without starting a single project (if you think you have the will power). Then go back to the beginning chapters that talk about equipment. When you're ready to tackle your first project, line up everything you'll need.

It's best to get all your ducks in a row (so to speak) so that you can quickly and efficiently work with the hot wax. If you have to, reread the specific section again. In this way, you'll have little firmer grasp of what needs to be done. You'll feel a little more confident.

As you encounter projects or ideas, be sure to reread the relevant sections at least once -- twice if you want. Don't be bashful about returning to these pages to read and reread them again!

In fact, print out certain sections that you may want to consult while you're making your candles. Have them on your counter along with all your other supplies, just like you would have your favorite recipe available for consulting when you're making a meal.

In the process of referring back to this book often, you'll discover that you're slowly becoming a candle making pro. But more than that I can guess that you'll also start to love this easy-to-do craft.

After you make your first candle, my bet is that you'll take a step back, take a good look at it and then display it someplace where everyone who steps foot in your house can admire it! That's what I did anyway!

This book introduces you to the various types of candles from paraffin to beeswax to gel. As you progress through these various projects, you'll also discover that your imagination gets fired up! You'll want to keep making these candles.

And you'll find yourself continuing, as your friends and

families stand in line for custom-made candles to suit the décor of their homes or for gifts for their friends and coworkers.

And you might possibly get fired up about spreading the word about candle making even more! You may end up considering it as a part-time business. Don't laugh! It's really not out of the question. Even if you just sold locally, you can make a nice income -- especially if you have unique versions of candles that people can't find in stores. Just keep it in mind as you read! The last chapter in this book provides you with some statistics on who actually uses candles, and where. It also provides you with some rudimentary marketing tips . . . enough to get you started should you decide to become that part-time entrepreneur.

Are you ready to discover a remarkably easy, extremely fun . . . and potentially profitable hobby?

Well, let's start then. Time's a'wastin'.

CHAPTER ONE:
History of Candles and Candle Making

Welcome! You're about to join a small, elite group of candle making lovers who enjoy a rich, illustrious heritage!

Today, we make candles for pure enjoyment! But, try to imagine back to more than hundred, even two hundred years ago, when candles weren't just a pleasant luxury.

Candles, prior to the advent of electricity, were a necessity -- they were used to provide the lighting for the house once the sun set. It's difficult -- if not impossible -- for us to truly imagine living without the convenience of a light switch to flood our living rooms with light.

Can you imagine how hard it must have been to carry out any activity by candle light alone -- let alone knit, crochet or even read by the small light of candles. (It's a wonder Abraham Lincoln didn't go blind!)

And yes, it's hard to imagine that if you wanted to wander from room to room in your own house after dark, you took a candle in some type of holder wherever you went.

But, now that you've pondered what many of us would consider the "downside" or disadvantages of living by candle light, let's look at some of the benefits of living by candle light.

Imagine this art of candle making being handed down from mother to daughter. Regularly, they would work together at making enough candles to last for a month or so. It must have been an incredibly satisfying task knowing that you were supplying your family with much needed light for the home.

The bright history of candles

It appears to be a continuing trait of mankind - a fascination with candles. Perhaps it harkens back to prehistoric times. A candle, after all, is in essence fire. And fire is one of the four great elements basic to life on earth, according to our early ancestors.
How often have you let your gaze shift to a candle flame or the flames of a fireplace? How often have the flames which have leapt from these been transformed into some imaginative figure? Fire, to the human mind, it seems, is so much more than just a mode to heat or to light a room. It's an invitation to reach beyond ourselves.

And how many of us think of candles as religious symbols? Many individuals to this day, think candles, and immediately think Christmas or Hanukkah.

Candle evolution

The truth of the matter is that mankind has used candles since the Stone Age. And ever since the Stone Age, man has marveled at the strength and power of the candle.

In fact, archeologists have discovered references to the candle as far back as 3,000 BC! For the most part, these candles have been found in Egypt as well as on the island of Crete in Greece.

While no candle itself has been discovered in ancient Egypt, clay candleholders dating to the fourth century BC have been discovered at various archaeological sites in this country.

The tomb of the famous pharaoh King Tutankhamen, opened in 1922, revealed a bronze candleholder among other ancient wonders. Archeologists now theorize that the ancient Egyptians may very well have been the first civilization to develop candles.

> **The oldest candle fragment archeologists have discovered dates from the first century A.D. It was unearthed near the town of Avignon, France.**

Don't think for a moment that ancient candles looked anything like the candles you're about to make. Because they didn't. But the ancient people were nothing if not ingenious in the creation of much needed light.

The first candles -- you wouldn't recognize them!

The first "candles" were called "rush lights" or "rush dips". The first differing element you'll notice is that the "rush lights" have no wicks. Instead, these candle-like items were probably made from rocks or stones which themselves contained a natural depressed area -- which acted as a cup.

Our ancient ancestors poured animal fat into this shape and something called a rush. A rush was nothing more than a straw-like plant material. It was pressed into the fat and then lit. Individuals quickly learned which material worked well and which didn't. Soon they discovered that oil from fruits, nuts and plants usually worked. Or in the warmer climates, like Italy. olive oil worked well.

Cultures that lived by the ocean also discovered that oil from marine life worked well for light. They soon created lamps specifically created to hold the fat or oil and its rush.
They were made of natural soft stone -- much like soapstone-- or sometimes clay. These individuals also believed fire to be a sacred element. The containers then, were treated with the utmost respect and caring devotion.

Animal fats fuel candles

The simple form of rush lights soon evolved into more sophisticated forms. Many of these rush lights were soon made with animal fats -- because people were slaughtering and eating more meat. Fats from animals soon became the common vehicle for lighting.

In fact, up until the 19th century, there were three basic types of animal fat commonly used for candles. This fat was called tallow and it came from beef fat, pork fat or mutton -- lamb fat.

Of the three, most people agree that mutton was by far the best. It burned longer, smoked very little and was the least odorous of the three.

Pork was unacceptable because it not only a produced a thick smoke, but it also gave off a terrible smell. If you knew nothing at all about a family's economic status, you could tell it from walking into their house and smelling their candles.

Those in the upper economic strata burned mutton -- the least smelly. The poor families had to settle to burning the smelliest of all the fats -- pig fat.

The growth of chandlers

Candle making wouldn't become recognizable to us until the 13th century. That's when itinerant candle makers traveled from village to town and door to door. Actually, these "chandlers" as they were called were very popular. There services were in such high demand that in Paris alone had more than 70 chandlers according to the tax list of 1292.

The chandlers erected their specialized candle making equipment. The clients would provide the material for the merchants who fashioned the candles.

As the number of these service providers grew, the chandlers eventually created guilds. These occurred in both England and Paris. The English Tallow Chandlers, for example, incorporated in 1462. They regulated trade in candles that were made from animal fat -- those made for the common person.

Those chandlers who specialized in wax catered to the upper class families. They also made more money. Only the wealthy could afford to buy wax.

Beeswax was also known as a good material for candles. But it for the most part was difficult with which to work. Until the invention of candle molds and stearin in the 1820s, in fact, all candles from beeswax had to be tailored by hand. This was extremely time consuming. Because of this, beeswax cand es were found chiefly in churches and monasteries.

And because of this, monasteries not only became great consumers of candles but great creators of them as well. Candle making was a common task, just like cooking and gardening.

The Catholic Church valued beeswax so much -- and it was so expensive -- that Catholics were allowed to pay their tithes to the church using this substance.

Lighting the streets

Beginning in the 1400s, candle lanterns lit the streets during the night hours. The town crier travelled the town at night, attending to all the candles and calling out the time: "11 o'clock and all's well!"

Prior to the lit streets, people wouldn't venture out at night, fearful of assault, robbery or some other type of attack. Only the brave left their houses at night. The brave or the aristocracy. The aristocracy could afford candlelit carriages, as well as servants to carry the candles ahead of these individuals as they walked.

The fifteenth century brought a new type of advancement in candles: the mold. Paris in particular was the center of wax chandlering and proved to be innovative at forming a guild.

The candle molds at this time though could only be used on tallow candles. When beeswax melted, it became very sticky. And it couldn't be removed from the molds. So beeswax candles continued, even in this century, to be a product for the Church only and continued to be constructed by hand.

A new use for candle light

With the advent of the 16th century, another valuable use was discovered for candles -- lighting theatrical performances -- not only plays, but pageants and musical events as well. In Italy, especially, indoor theater became very popular.

The theater of this era utilized the common light sources of the day -- including tallow candles. But even in Shakespeare's England, were lit by candles, especially in the winter.

Candle making changes of revolutionary proportions

Perhaps no era of history reminds us of candles as much as the colonial era of U.S. history. When we think of the time just prior to the Revolutionary War, candles seem to be one of the first items that come to mind. Why even during the war, the cry from Old North Church in Boston involved the lighting of candles, "One if by land, two if by sea."

The warning of how the British would attack would be signaled through the use of . . . . candles!

The itinerant chandler, as found so prevalently in many parts of Europe, was scarce in the U.S. Making candles became part of the normal household function, performed by the wives and daughters.

More often than not, it was an event that only occurred

once a year, designed to coincide with the yearly slaughtering of the family's farm animals.

> **"A tallow candle, to be good, must be half Sheep's Tallow and half Cow's; that of hogs mekes 'em gutter, give an ill smell, and a thick black smoak."**
> *~An observation (and advice) from an anonymous 18th century source*

Colonial America and candle making

Candle making in the New World was indeed just as hot, tedious and smelly as it had been in Europe, yet, we seem to have romanticized the entire process. And since the process only occurred once a year, the entire procedure turned into quite an event.

Consider that within several days to a week's time, the creation of 200 to 400 candles to last your family throughout the entire year! That's about the number of candles the average colonial family burned in twelve months' time.

So it's not surprising -- given that it was a yearly event that every woman in the town or village did -- that eventually it became a social event as well. Women soon learned to pull their resources together and socialize at the same time (considering the amount of work to be performed in a single day, how often did you get a chance to visit Martha or Jane?

For the average family, the most inexpensive mode of creation was through dipping candles. Wealthier homes, though, may have owned a candle mold made of wood or tin. Of course, the molds greatly increased the speed of the creation itself.

It didn't take long for chandlers to appear in this country. As the economy strengthened families could better afford to pay a chandler to make the candles, instead of spending the better part of a week or so creating them.

Eventually, though, families depended neither on the yearly candle making time nor on chandlers. They eventually were able to buy candles at the local apothecary.

A unique contribution

Imagine a house lit by candle light. Of course, we consider it romantic. But, I want you to really imagine what it must have been like -- especially when the candles were created from tallow. Romance seems to rush out the door when you consider that the candles smelled like sheep fat or beef!

So it must have seemed quite revolutionary (if you don't mind me using that phrase) when colonial America discovered the lovely smelling bayberry created a perfect wax for burning. Colonial women, no doubt disgusted by the smell of tallow clogging up their homes, and realizing that beeswax would never be within their financial reach sought other materials for candles.

What better choice than bayberry! Women of colonial America discovered - we're not quite sure the exact route! -- that these grayish green berries found on the bayberry bush could be boiled down. The boiling process left a lovely-smelling wax.

Of course, there was just one small glitch in the process: *It took approximately 15 pounds of bayberries to create one pound of bayberry wax.* That s a whole lot of berry picking!

A second glitch soon appeared as well. Bayberry candles did not hold up well under storage. After only a few months of being stored, colonial wives noticed that a white powdery residue formed on the candles. They referred to this as "blooming."

Bayberry candles soon became a seasonal candle, since they couldn't be used on a daily basis. These sweet-smelling creations grew in popularity especially at Christmas time.

Candles and . . . whales

You knew I was bound to get there. Cows may have fat . . . and certainly pigs have fat -- and sheep as we're learning have the least offensive smelling fat.

But nothing says fat . . . well, like a whale (Sorry, Shamu!)

And it just so happened that the early American colonists became adept at whaling. By the 1700s, a considerably profitable whaling industry had grown on the coast. And it didn't take long after that before colonists began making candles from this immense creature.

Specifically, colonists discovered the oil in the head of the sperm whale created the best candles. These became known as spermaceti candles or spermaceti wax. As you might imagine, however, even these candles didn't smell all that good! (No kidding!)

But most colonists agreed that the smell was better than tallow from the farm animals. Not only that, but this particular wax produced a harder candle which didn't lose its shape even in the hottest part of the summer. And spermaceti wax had the added advantage of being less expensive than beeswax.

The spermaceti candle, however, was never a home-made piece of lighting.. it was also manufactured and sold to consumers. In fact, shortly after the Revolutionary War, the economic fortunes of Nantucket, MA shone bright as a candle, when it became the home of just about all spermaceti candle-making in the young country.

Perhaps the largest -- and most revolutionary -- changes to candle usage occurred along with the advent of the Industrial Revolution, starting from 1750 and continuing for the next century. The entire economic structure of the world changed drastically during this period.

The advent of the candle molding machines

Developments spurred by the overall development of the Industrial Revolution exerted great changes in the world of making candles. One of the largest changes involved the creation of molding machines invented during the first portion of the 19th century.

Another aspect that proved to be revolutionary for this activity was the invention of the braided wick. Developed by a French gentleman, named

Cambaceres, this development solved one of the largest problems of candles during this period. Wicks burned in an uneven fashion; they needed to be "snuffed" or trimmed while they were burning.

With the braided wick, one thread in this braid wick was tighter than the other two. It in effect, the wick now became "self trimming" as it burned. While it may seem like a small matter, it really created quite a stir. Braided wicks burned more efficiently than the non-braided version.

But there were still drawbacks. Making candles, admittedly, was a slow, labor-intensive process. There were, after all, only so many candles on chandler could churn out in a day.
Ah! But all that was about to change, thanks to the mind of Joseph Morgan. An Englishman, he invented a machine in 1834 that could make molded candles at the unbelievable rate of 1,500 in one hour. And the machine could "wick" continuously.

Life was about to change drastically for everyone! In effect, Morgan had discovered a method to "mass produce" candles. Now, to you and me this might not be a momentous occasion, but it was about to turn the world of the typical 19th century person on its head!

For the first time ever, candles became an affordable product, to just about everyone! In the same year the mold machine came into use, the "mordanting" process was also introduced.

Never hear of the "mordanting" process? This, too, was a major breakthrough. Mordanting-soaking the wick became popular. This meant that the wick was placed in an acid-like solution which allowed the wick to curl at a 90 degree angle away from the pool of melted wax, away from the flame zone -- where it turned to ash.

Introducing paraffin wax, another revolutionary concept

As if these two developments weren't enough, two more events melted together which only promulgated the popularity as well as the ease of using candles. Paraffin was introduced in 1850. This artificial commercially manufactured wax, proved to be a welcome alternative to tallow -- the less than fragrant animal fat.

Soon after this, chemist Michel Eugene Chevreul discovered the true nature of tallow. It wasn't composed of just one substance. It was created out of two distinct fatty acids -- stearic and oleic acids. From this discovery, he created a completely new substance known as stearin. When added to paraffin, stearin produced a harder, opaque, longer-burning candle.

This made candles affordable and abundant! It, in effect, creating candle making as we know it today. Factory-made candles surged in popularity. Candle making by hand though was soon to pass the way of the dodo bird -- a thing of the past.

Stronger, longer-burning candles

Consider it candle's golden age. It were as if the world suddenly discovered the "bionic candle" -- "We can make it stronger, better, longer-burning!" And indeed candle manufacturers did!

But still, there's something to be said for making your

own candles. And the next chapter equips you with all the tools of the trade you'll need!

> "Thousands of candles can be lit from a single candle, and the life of the candle will not be shortened. Happiness never decreases by being shared." Buddha

CHAPTER TWO:
Candle Making Supplies:
Taking Stock of Your Stock

Every good craftsman has some basic tools of the trade as they're called. The master carpenter has his hammer, for example. The master mason has his trowel. Whether you realize it or not, you're about to join the ranks of the master craftsperson. And you, too, should have one or two basic tools of your "trade" or craft.

Okay, so perhaps you want to downplay the "master" portion of the phrase -- at least for now. Give yourself some time, though. Before you know it, you'll be producing those exquisite candles.

Let's face it, the fundamentals of candle making are pretty simple to grasp. You take hard wax, melt it down, reshape it, stick a wick in it and let it sit and re-harden. Pretty easy. (This is even easier if you use beeswax, because that type of wax doesn't even need to be melted down -- wait till you read about that!)

As crafts go, its ease ranks right up there with . . . well, I really don't think it get easier than this. And the end result certainly doesn't get any more beautiful than this.

That means the "equipment" involved in creating these stylish pieces is kept to a minimum. Here's what you need to make your first candles:

1. A heat source.

A heat source is nothing more than your kitchen range or a hot pot of some kind. One word of caution here, don't use a microwave. At tempted as you might be, the temperature variations of this appliance aren't suited to the precision of melting wax.

2. A pot.

You'll need a container in which to melt your wax. Preferably, you'll want to use a double boiler or something that will substitute for a double boiler. If you don't have a double boiler, you may want to place empty cans on the bottom of a large pot arranged so that a smaller pot can nestle sturdily in there.

Or you can find two pots and simply place the smaller one inside the larger one.

The pan which is directly touching the heat source will be filled with water which will heat up to eventually, evenly and slowly melt the wax in the second pan. You'll want to keep the smaller pan, by the way, at least a half inch above the base of the larger pot.

There's only once exception to using double boiler. That's gel wax. The temperature at which gel wax gets "syrupy" (because it never really melts in the traditional sense) is between 200 and 220 degrees. You can't reach this temperature with a double boiler.

So keep in mind, when you think you're ready to work with this type of material that a double boiler isn't needed (I'll remind you again when we get to that section) and be extremely alert to all safety concerns.

3. Thermometer.

Since wax melts quickly and has the very real potential to literally explode if it reaches too high a temperature, you'll discover that a thermometer is an absolute necessity. If you don't use one specifically created for candles, you can use a candy thermometer or any one which indicates temperatures ranging from 100 to 300 degrees Fahrenheit.

Whatever you do, don't try to "eyeball" the temperature of your wax. If you've ever made candy, you may have discovered you got good at just looking at the texture of the candy to discern its temperature. Wax is well . . . a whole different ball of wax . . . in this department.

4. Candle molds.

Molded candles are usually the easiest for novice candle makers to create. Be sure to have these ready to fill if your first project is to be this type. In a little bit, I'll fill you in on the other options of candle varieties you can create. Just be sure whatever type you're planning on using, to have it ready to go before you start you project.

If you keep the following, small piece of knowledge in mind, you should not only be a successful candle maker, but a true lover of the art. Take a lesson from the Boy Scouts: **Be prepared!** It'll make your project go that much easier! (And I certainly speak from experience on this one!)

5. Dipping Can

When you choose dipping taper candles, you'll want some type of metal container that's wide enough and tall enough in which to dip your candles.

Of course, you can purchase one specially created for this task. But you may just find something suitable you already have at home. If that's the case, then by all means use it!

In fact, if your melting pot is at least 12 inches wide, you won't even need to worry about a separate dipping can. You've got it right there! (Yes, I said wide. Let me clue you in on one quick aspect of dipping. The first one or two times you dip that wick into the wax, it just might not sink well for you. It might float because it lacks enough weight. Don't worry after a while your candle and the weight of the wax will cause it to sink.)

That's all you need for the simplest of projects. As you continue with your newfound hobby -- and you can feel it, continue with it you will! -- you may want to add to your "necessary equipment."

6. Kitchen scale

Eventually, you may want to weigh your wax and wax additive to ensure you're using the proper amount for consistent results. The optimum scale is a digital postal scale. This is more accurate than a spring-type diet scale -- especially when it comes to weighing those additives and fragrances. But keep in mind the digital postal scale is also a little more expensive as well.

7. Baking pan

This is extremely handy when it comes time to clean your molds. Just line the backing pan with aluminum foil. As you clean these, keep close watch on the temperature you use. If you heat them for two long, they may begin to melt!

8. Scissors, razor blade, craft knife

The decision is yours. But you'll soon learn that you'll need some type of cutting instrument. Sharp tools help you to trim your wick, and cut your wax.
When you cut off the amount of wax you need from your block of wax, make sure you have protection for your countertop. It's far too easy for the sharp object to accidently cut clear through the wax and right onto your countertop.

9. Hammer and screwdriver

Sometimes, you may need to break your slabs of wax apart, depending on its size. The easiest way to do this is to pretend you're a sculptor. Take the screwdriver and place it in the wax. Then you simply hammer the end of the screwdriver to create the break in the wax. Again, just as a protective measure, you may want to put something underneath this chunk of wax to protect your kitchen counter.

10. Mold sealers

You may also hear these refer to as wick sealers. They're the same item. These are used to close up the hole where you threaded in your wick. In this way the wax won't leak out!

11. Releasing agent or mold releases

This is a special silicone spray expressly made as a releasing agent. Found at just about all craft stores, this spray is applied sparingly to the inside of the mold, much like vegetable oil is applied to a cake pan when baking. It helps to make removal of the finished product from the mold easier. In fact, if you don't have a mold release, you may substitute vegetable oil -- it works just as well! If you have some vegetable oil spray . . . well, this is even better!

12. Wax glue

This is used to apply designs, embellishments and other pieces of wax to the sides of your candles.

13. Wick tabs

These are thin metal bases that you attach to the

bottom of your wick if your wick is untabbed. An untabbed wick, by the way, is simply a wick missing that thin metal base which anchors it in the candle and helps it to stand straight.

Usually used in votive and container candles, the tabs are also used in molds that don't have a hole in the bottom.

14. Fire extinguisher

Yes! A fire extinguisher. It's much better to be safe than sorry. Hopefully, you'll never need to use it. But please be careful and have on close by.

Candle making clean up

Let's face it, accidents are going to happen. This is especially true if you've taken on the hobby of candle making as a family affair. Heck, we adults even have our moments. And some of our "best moments" (aka most disastrous!) occur when we do everything in our power to be as careful as possible.

If you make candles long enough, you're bound to create the dreaded "wax spill." It actually sounds a lot worse than what it is. A wax spill is usually fairly easy to clean -- if you know what to do.

No matter what type of wax you should happen to spill, the basic treatment of the spill is essentially the same.

Of course, let me say right from the start, that as a result of a hot wax spill that has touched you, your skin is blistering, call your personal health-care practitioner immediately. The blistering indicates you have a very serious burn -- and it needs immediate medical attention.

If you're not blistering, the pain is not overwhelming and you believe it's "treatable" at home, then immediately place the affected body part in cool water. Never put any part of your body burnt by a wax spill in cold water. The extreme range in temperature you'd be subjecting your skin too may send it into shock.

When the wax cools (This shouldn't take very long at all), gently peel the wax off your skin. Now you can treat the burn like any other burn. You may use calamine lotion or aloe vera on the affected area. Never use butter.

If you spill melted gel wax on you, the gel is a little more difficult to get off your skin. The longer it stays on in fact, the more it continues to burn.

If the wax is on something other than your body, wait until it hardens before you attempt to clean it up. Trying to clean it while it's still melted just creates a bigger mess (Yes, if you must know, I speak from experience on this one!)

If you feel the need to speed the process along, rub an ice cube on the wax to help it cool. If the item is moveable or pliable, like clothing, you can even place it in the freezer to speed the cooling process.

You've got all your candle-making supplies in a row -- and you're ready to start making some beautiful candles. Well, not quite. Sorry to burst your bubble. You still need to know a little bit about what every candle needs to burn brightly . . . and fragrantly . . .

and beautifully.

I'm talking about wicks, fragrance and dyes. And it's time to introduce you to the various types of waxes from which you can choose. What? You thought there was just one type of wax. No way! How boring would that be!

CHAPTER THREE:
What Every Candle Needs:
Wax, Wick, Color, and Scent

Four elements compose your standard -- and even your fancy -- candle. Wax, wick, color and scent.

Of course you could argue that the scent is not a necessity. And that's true. A candle shines just as bright whether it smells sweetly or not -- that just happens to be an added benefit.

And eventually as you evolve from novice candle maker to experienced chandler, you'll, at some point, want to include in your "portfolio" a scented candle or two. So it doesn't hurt to talk about it now, even if it's a while before you actually make a fragrant candle.

And color, well, by the time you're done making your second candle that's just "paraffin white" you'll be ready to experiment with colors. And you'll love what you can do with them! Guaranteed.

But for now, let's just go over the basic elements of a candle . . .

Wax On . . . About Waxes

Ah! Let's talk for a moment about the most essential ingredient in this entire process of candle making -- the main ingredient -- the type of wax you choose.

Three crucial elements affect the outcome and the quality of your project: the type of wax you use, the amount of wax and its temperature when you're melting it.

Here we'll just talk about the differences in waxes. For now, this gives you a background for your first wax-shopping trip. You'll probably start with the most common of waxes -- the paraffin-based wax. This is the wax most people use, at least initially.

As you master the first steps in candle making -- and discover just how easy it is -- you'll be venturing out to other types of waxes before you know it.

Blended paraffin and paraffin waxes

These are probably the types of waxes from which you'll fashion your first project. These are petroleum-based waxes and can be found in a variety of blends. One of the benefits of using this type of medium is it produces an odorless smoke.

The melting point of this wax varies between 104 and 160 degrees. The actual temperature at which the paraffin you buy melts depends in large part on its quality.

Later we talk about additives. One of these is stearin. Many candle makers add this to their candles. You may also find that the wax you buy already has this in it. The package contents will tell you this. If you're not sure at the time you buy your wax, ask the staff at the craft store at which you bought it. If they don't know offhand, they'll find someone who does.

Bead wax

Granulated into small beads, this type of wax can be

found in a variety of colors and scents. And it has a convenience factor that you may find refreshing.

You can incorporate bead wax into your candle making hobby in one of two ways (or use both at different times!). You can simply melt it instead of the chunky paraffin wax.

Or you can add it whole to another melted wax to create a great, new colorful design. If you want the beads to retain their spherical shape, add them when the base wax is cooling and less likely to distort their shape.

How do you melt bead wax? The same way that you melt any other wax. Definitely use a double boiler! The advantage of this type of wax though is the relatively uniform shape of the beads. And because the beads are smaller and more uniform, you can calculate a more accurate measurement of the wax you'll need for your project.

Adding beads of different colors of beads to your base color creates the most festive-looking of candles. You can add pizzazz to any candle this way. Think about a Christmas candle using red and green beads. Or use just green beads and call it a St. Patrick's Day candle!

In honor of Easter and the pastel colors usually used in this season, use a variety of spring, pastel colors to create a gorgeous Easter candle.

Well, I don't need to go any further, because I can see your imagination is already working.

Beeswax

This natural wax, comes in blocks or sheets. It can also be bought as natural, unbleached or bleached white. Beeswax possesses a natural honey fragrance. And many candle makers like to add it to a paraffin mix base because it lengthens the burning time of the candle.

Beeswax burns slower than paraffin. It's natural golden color is a delight to behold. Some individuals though bleach it so it's white. The choice, ultimately, will be yours and will undoubtedly depend on the needs of your project.

But remember if your candle wax ends up to be more than 10 percent beeswax, it just might be tough removing the candle from the mold when your project is completed.

If you're trying to save money, then you probably don't want to buy beeswax. It costs more than paraffin. And if you're still a novice you may want to postpone your entry into making candles with melted pure beeswax because of the problems it presents getting it out of molds.

If you're not using molds and instead you're creating container candles, then you may want to try it.

> **You can't light a candle to show others the way without feeling the warmth of that bright little ray . . .**
>
> ~Unknown

You can purchase beeswax in two forms: granular or in sheets. Buying beeswax in sheets has one distinct advantage. To make a pure beeswax taper candle, you don't need to melt the wax. Simple wrap it around a primed wick. Yeah, it really is that easy! (What a great way to get even the youngest of children involved with you without the worry of melted wax!)

Working with beeswax does have one drawback. They don't mix with the fragrance additives very well. A candle made of beeswax just isn't going to smell like one made of paraffin. So if the scent of the candle is important to you or for a special reason (such as an aromatherapy candle) you definitely don't want to use this type of wax.

Soy wax

While we're talking about natural wax, I'd be remiss if I didn't mention the latest entry into the world of candle making: soy wax!

Wait! No, you don't eat soy wax. You melt it! But you're right! It is made from soy beans. Go figure! (But, I'm betting it couldn't taste any worse than tofu!)

Soy wax has been part of the candle making family now for a little more than a decade. But in those 10 years or so it has filled a void. More candle makers are searching for natural materials with which to create candles. The only material up until this point has been beeswax -- and that type of wax can be expensive if it's the only type of wax you use.

Specifically soy wax is made from hydrogenated soybean oil. See, I told you that you really didn't want to eat this wax! In addition to being all natural and less expensive than beeswax, soy wax is environmentally friendly -- at least more than it cousin paraffin wax.

Not only that, but soy wax melt more slowly than paraffin. Because of this a soy candle lasts about 50 percent longer than a paraffin candle of the same size. Soy candles also produce less soot (that black residue that we continually wash off our candle holders).

If those weren't enough benefits to using soy, this type of wax also distributes scents easier. Oh? Did I mention that clean up after accidental spills is also much easier with this natural wax? It is. All you need to use is soap and water.

Container candles

Soy's low melting point makes it the ideal wax for container candles. You may want to try your hand initially at creating soy candles in canning jars.

And don't worry about what kind of wicks you'll need. Soy takes the same types of wicks as paraffin candles do. You may want to make sure that you use a tab on your wick, though. This will help it to adhere to the bottom of the jar.

Whether you buy pre-tabbed wick or purchase the tabs separately is completely up to you. Placing the tab on the wick is easy enough (in case you discover you don't have any pre-tabbed wicks available when you start a soy project). You simply thread the wick through the tab, then squeeze the tabs so the wick is immobile.

Another big advantage to using soy wax as the basis of your candles is the method of melting the wax. That's right! You can melt soy over direct heat.

Gel wax

This is merely clear gel and can be found at just about any local craft store. This is fun to work with because you may drop small decorative items into the gel to make stunningly beautiful and individually tailored gifts for friends and family.

But of all the candle waxes available to you, this may be the most dangerous to work with as well. Because of the hotter melting point, you'll need to put this wax directly over a heat source -- and be very careful.

The key to working with gel wax is remembering that it won't "melt" for you in the traditional sense. When you work with paraffin, you'll notice that your chunk of wax goes from one physical state -- that of a chunk (or chunks) of wax -- to a melted or molten form.

The transformation of gel wax won't be quite as definite. The gel, as it gets hotter, it comes to resemble a syrup-like substance more and more. If you continue to melt it, thinking that it's going to get thinner . . . well . . . that just won't happen.

But many candle makers love to work with it because it's clear. And that means you have just about an unlimited choice of adding accessories to create beautiful images.

Wax chunks

These chunks come in a broad variety of colors. You can melt these individual pieces when you only need a small portion of wax. Or you can keep them as they are and embed them into a larger candle to make a unique look.

Or you can look at these chunks of wax and say -- like many other candle makers have in the past: "I can make chunks in the exact size and color I like."

Want to know how?

If you have a baking or a cookie sheet with sides, you can begin! In fact, take this baking sheet and line it with aluminum foil. Make sure you even line the sides of the pan with the foil as well. Got it? Good!

Depending on how big you want you chunks, shape your foil so your baking sheet container is taller than it is wide. If you want smaller chunks, then keep the foil lined with the natural sides of the pan.

Wax chunks don't have to be huge to have a beautiful impact on your candle creation.

Now, melt your wax in a double boiler just as if you were making a candle. Once your wax is melted thoroughly pour it into your pouring pot. Instead of pouring this into a mold or container, you're take the molten wax in the pouring pot and pour it as evenly as possible on your baking sheet.

Allow this to cool completely. Once it has, you can then cut the wax into the exact size chunks you want for your next project. It's as easy as that.

What's a Candle Without A Wick?

Indeed, what is a candle without a wick? In a word: useless! Unless you have that wick to light, your candle is just . . . well, a large, beautiful piece of hard wax.

And it's not going to provide you the hours of glittering lit beauty if you can't light it.

Before your candle making experiences, you may not have thought much about wicks. But I assure you, by the time you've finished reading this book and making a few candles, you'll be the wick expert on your block!

A wick selection is not an event to be performed frivolously. In fact, the farther along you delve into this craft, the more involved you'll be in deciding on just the right wick for your project.

Wick selection involves several wide-ranging variables, including the type of wax you're using, the ultimate size of your candle (or its diameter or width), the fragrance oil density and your own personal preferences.

Now, having said all that, you may think that choosing a wick is a bit intimidating. Nothing however is farther from the truth. It may be a bit challenging for you at the beginning, but as soon as you make a selection or two, it'll become second nature for you.

If you want, as you advance in your project making, you may want to jot down some notes concerning the wick size, wax type, the pour temperature as well as the diameter and the fragrance type you used with what types of wicks.

In this way, you can note whether the performance of the wick was adequate or not. If it was, you'll know exactly what type you want when you repeat that project or a similar one.

If the wick didn't perform well, then you'll know *what not to use* the next time around.

You'll soon discover that there's a great deal of "working science" at work in your wick. And as you become more proficient at choosing wicks, you'll become something of a "wick expert." Imagine that!

For now, keep in that the diameter of a wick matters. If you select a wick that is too thick or chunky for your size candle, the result is a flame that a burns too brightly. And that in turns, means your candle burns far too quickly. This is not an efficient use of your candle. But more than that, it's also a hazard.

Choose a wick that's too thin and the opposite occurs. The candle burns too slowly or gently. Only the inner portion of your candle melts. The wax, in effect, saturates the wick and all burning stops.

Typically, you'll discover that candle wicks are sold braided. This isn't for a nice look. Braided wicks, for one thing, helps to indicate the thickness of the wick itself. The more braids a wick possesses, the thicker it is.

Cotton Core wicks

These wicks have a rigid inner core which aids in it standing straight while burning. Some candle making specialists believe that the cotton core wicks are perfect for working with soy and paraffin. These same people believe that, on the whole, this specific wick "mushrooms" less than others. "Mushrooming" causes an increase in soot production because of its carbon guil up.

Flat braid wicks

This particular type of wick is neither waxed nor tabbed. You may want to consider their use with pillar candles or even tapers. Flat braid wicks are more "self trimming" than square braid ones.

Square braid wicks contain a core of rigid zinc. This enables them to stay straight while in the melted wax. Zinc core wicks are popular and they are easy to use. One of the disadvantages of this wick though is its tendency to "mushroom." You can easily overcome this, many candle making fans say, by ensuring you have chosen the proper size of the wick as well by trimming the wick.

Zinc core wicks are recommended from use in paraffin and gel waxes.

Wire core wicks

This particular wick is especially effective when you're making container nd votive candles. It has a metal wire center, whicha llos the wick to stand upright in its melted wax.

Prime wick?

Primed or unprimed? That is the question. Oh, excuse me. It's hard to give a good answer to that question if you're not quite sure what the difference is between these two types of wicks.

When you go to buy your first bag of wicks, you'll notice that you have a choice: primed or unprimed. And the first time you see this, you may stand there for a while wondering which to buy.

And if you have luck like I had, your first wick purchase will be wrong. But then, I didn't have the aid of a book like this to at least give me some idea of what to use. I hope this helps you -- even a little.

If you choose to work with soy, you're going to want to choose a primed wick.

Don't panic if you look at your packages of wick and they're all unprimed. There's an easy way to correct this. You can prime the wick yourself! Yes, you! It's not a challenging act at all, as you're about to see.

A primed wick may be essential in certain projects because it ensures a more even burn of your candle. A wick that's primed also lights with greater ease and burns more reliably.

But that's not all, when you use a primed wick you don't have to worry about moisture or water. Priming the wick helps to keep both of these from being absorbed by the wick.

The first difference between the two is the rigidity of the wicks. A primed wick is stiffer and more rigid than an unprimed one. And this quality is why they're so useful. Being more rigid, they're able to stand upright in the candle with greater ease.

When you prime a wick, you simply dip it into melted wax until it's completely coated. You then remove the wick from the wax, and let it harden. Once the wax has hardened, you dip the wick back into the melted wax a second time. You again let this harden. Then you may use the wick or simply store it until you need it.

Using primed wicks is a great habit to cultivate. Even though you have the instructions for priming a wick in a nutshell, I'm including step by step instructions for you. After a while, I'm sure you'll become a pro at this, but I know that the first several times you prime your wick, you'll feel more comfortable following a step-by-step outline.

Easy Steps to Wick Priming

What you'll need:

1. Wicks
2. Thermometer
3. Double boiler
4. Aluminum foil or waxed paper

Priming Step #1

Heat your wax in a double boiler. (I've already provided you with good double boiler instructions in Chapter 2, just follow these!) This time around though you're not going to heat as much wax as for a candle. Use only a small amount, you only want to get the wicks coated in it.

Priming Step #2:

Check the temperature of your wax as you burn it. Again, you're looking for a temperature of between 150 and 160 degrees F.

Once you have the desired temperature, carefully tip the pan containing the wax away from you, so the melted material gathers in one end of the bottom of the wax.

While holding onto the end of the wick, dip it into the molten wax. Do not drop the wick into the wax. (Don't make that silly mistake like I did!)

Keep the wick in the wax until air bubbles surface. This

will take -- under normal circumstances -- about 30 seconds. The appearance of the air bubbles indicate that the wick has absorbed enough wax and you can remove it from the wax.

Priming Step #3

Lay the wick gently on wax paper. Pull it tautly. Now don't touch it again until it hardens. This will take only a few minutes. Once it does occur you can use it!

Before you even use the wick, remember to cut the small section you were hold and didn't receive any wax. Now you have a completely primed wick. And you did it yourself! Congratulations, Craftsperson!

Here's One Prime Tip:

Some chandlers -- as those who make candles are called -- sometimes choose to prime each individual wick twice. Yes, just like you think. Once the wick of the initial dunking has hardened, these individuals choose to repeat the entire process.

Some of these same folks also hang their wicks for drying instead of laying them out on aluminum foil or wax paper. If you choose this, it's easy enough to do. Simply tie a knot at the end of the wick. In this way you'll have a loop on which to hang the wick.

Even though you haven't asked . . .

. . . I feel compelled to explain it to you. What? How a wick really works. Actually, it's really quite fascinating (even though not essential to your immediate candle making requirements!).

Two parts come together to create a burning candle. The first is the fuel, which, of course, is the wax. The second, equally important, is the wick, which is made of one of the materials I've mentioned above.

All of the wick materials, you'll notice (or perhaps haven't, but I'll tell you) are naturally absorbent, much like a towel that sops up spills. If the material itself isn't naturally absorbent, then it needs to have something called a "strong capillary action."

The next time you buy a wick at a craft store that is not waxed, buy several extras, and give them a good inspection -- that is play with them. Take them in your hands and just examine them thoroughly. You'll soon discover that it feels more like a soft string than anything else. If you ran water over it, you'd also discover that it absorbs it very nicely.

And it's just this absorbency power that is vital in the candle burning process. The wick must be able to absorb liquid wax. But more than that, the wick must absorb the wax and move it upward while the candle is burning.

Once you light that wick, you are actually melting the wax in and near it. The wick, then absorbs the liquid wax, pulling it upward. The heat of that flame then vaporizes the wax. It's actually the wax vapor that burns.

The wick itself really doesn't burn. The vaporizing wax cools the exposed wick, which, in effect, protects it.

Dying to Dye Your Candles?

Love to add some color to your candles, but aren't

quite sure how. Yep, I understand: you're "dying" to dye your candles. Okay, so prosecute me for the bad pun. You really didn't expect me to pass that one up, did you?

The point, though, is very important. A world of white candles would be pretty boring. So why should you limit yourself to making only white candles. Let's add some variety into this hobby, shall we?

Take your pick! Candle making dyes are found in a wide array of forms, including chips, flakes, liquid and powders. And it goes without saying that you can find them in just about any color you want.

Don't forget though that is you can't find the exact color you're looking for, you can also blend these colors to create even more beautiful shades (who says we aren't creative?)

Before you get too excited about the variety of dyes available to you -- and colors from which to choose, read these tips about handling dyes.

1. Handle all dyes carefully.

Some plastic equipment and even some clothing (Yikes!) may become permanently stained (Pretty in Permanent Pink?) when it comes in contact with certain dyes.

Before using any dye, check to see if there are general instructions or any advisory details. Then be sure to follow all the tips for both safety and stains for the type of dye you're using.

2. Don't overheat the dye.

Overheating the dye can cause color distortion. The ill effect may not be discernable immediately (bummer!) but it may take a few days to show up (gives new meaning to the color Burnt Sienna, now doesn't it?).

3. Don't use too much of the dye.

Some of us have a tendency to think that if a little is good, then more must be even better. It doesn't always work like that. Too much dye in your project can actually adversely affect your candle's burning qualities.

4. How to make a black candle.

If you find yourself either needing or desiring a black candle, heed this bit of advice. Don't start with a clear wax. Instead use pieces of scrap wax of various colors, then add black to this mixture as needed. You'll get a much better result.

Scent-sational
The scent of a candle

It's so true! Nothing smells sweeter than the scent of a candle. Some of us enjoy the scent while it's burning, providing that lovely low lighting; others seem to be able to discern the fragrance as the candle is extinguished.
And there's no doubt about it, once the candle has filled the room with that wonderfully sensational fragrance, it changes the entire atmosphere of not only the room, but of your own mood as well.

Where once you may have been agitated and upset,

you can't help find yourself feeling a little calmer. You're looking at the world now through a little friendlier eyes now.

Or you may find that a certain fragrance of a candle as energizing. When you come home from a long, tiring day at work, there's nothing better to catch your second wind with the fragrance coming from a candle -- especially a candle you made yourself!

If you want to your home-made creations tc have that of effect on you as well as others, then you'll have to check out the range of fragrences available to you.

Candle fragrances come in several forms: liquid, natural herbs, and solid wax perfume chips. But that's only the start of your choices. You have nearly an endless array of fragrances from which to choose. All you need to do is click on to an internet site to see what's available to you. Scents as varied as summer rain to Amish harvest to candied apples.

There's not need to settle for uninspiring candles any more! Not with the choices that abound everywhere.

Two Scen(t)Sational Tips

1. **Wait until you're just about ready to pour your melted wax into the pouring pot before adding your scent.**

This act keeps evaporation to a minimum. In this way, you can actually use less fragrance and enjoy it more!

2. **Don't add too much scent.**

It's a common mistake -- especially for those of us who

are new to the art. I know I certainly made this mistake (several times over!) when I began making candles. Adding too much the fragrance may cause mottling or pitting to the candle wax itself. Not only does this detract from the attractiveness of your candle, but it also makes it harder to remove your candle from the mold.

CHAPTER 4:
The Basic Steps And Troubleshooting Common Problems

Once you start making candles, this "synchronicity" effect occurs. You begin noticing candles everywhere you go. You'd swear that there are more candles in the world. That's probably not true, but you certainly are more aware of the candles there are!

And the majority of those candles, it's safe to say were made through one process: the mold.

Professional candle makers use sturdy molds, specifically designed for candle making. And no doubt as you go along, you'll find some wonderful molds at your local craft store or on the internet.

But if you're eager to get started (and I know you are) you may just want to use some items you have around the house. An empty tin can makes a great mold, as does a cardboard half-gallon milk container. Don't think you need to fill this to the entire volume of half-gallon with wax, though.

You can easily cut this carton so it's only half of its original height. And then you don't even need to fill that all the way. After all, it's your project, your candle, your imagination. Most importantly, it's your decision. Have fun with it.

Some individuals start off using "Pringles" potato chip cartons, others use just about anything that will hold hot wax. When you're deciding on your mold, however, just keep safety uppermost in your mind. Don't choose a mold which you know won't stand up to the heat of the wax. You'll just have a mess on your hands in the way of clean up -- and someone may get injured when the mold itself melts.

Once you've decided on your mold, then there's not a thing in the world preventing you from starting. So, here are your basic instructions for making a candle from a mold.

My suggestion is to read these instructions over once, to give yourself a good overview of how the process works. Then, it's a good idea to set out everything you're going to need, from the original chunk of wax you plan to melt, to your double boiler to the wicks and scents (if you plan to use one at first). Also print the pages with these instructions out, if you have a printer, and refer to them as you go through the candle making process.

Once you have all of those supplies and the equipment within reach as well as the instructions not too far from you, it's time to start your candle making project.

Have fun!

Safety Tip:

Before you begin melting wax, make sure a working fire extinguisher is within easy reach. I'm really not trying to frighten you, but I want to give you a realistic outlook on the potential dangers of melting wax.

Wax is not like chicken soup. You don't put it on the

stove and walk away from it. You never leave melting wax unattended -- ever. Let me clue you in on one aspect of melting wax right away. The time it takes for the wax to melt from its original solid state seems as if it takes forever.

But once you get that wax to start the melting process, it begins to liquefy, the temperature rises quickly -- very quickly. It's just a safety tip head ups!

Getting Started:
Making A Basic Mold Candle

1. Place the block of wax into a large plastic bag. Then you place this on a large, solid surface. Using your hammer and screwdriver, break the wax into smaller pieces capable of fitting into the top of your double boiler.

2. Ensure the top section of your double boiler is deep enough to accommodate the length of a thermometer. You don't want its bulb to touch the bottom of the pan. Once you've done this, place the wax into the top section of the double boiler.

3. Fill the bottom of the double boiler with water. Put the top part of the double boiler on the bottom section. Don't forget to regularly check the bottom portion as the pan gets heated and the melting process progresses to ensure that the water doesn't completely evaporates.

4. Place the double boiler (or your version of a double boiler) on the heating element. Bring the water to a boil. Wax will slowly begin to melt, steadily liquefying.

5. Place your candle thermometer into the melting wax. Reduce the source of your heat to medium low. If the water in the double boiler begins to boil rapidly, reduce the heat again. At this point, all you want is for the water to be at a "gentle boil." If the water is boiling too rapidly, you are in danger of the water splashing up into the wax itself -- and this is not a situation that you don't want. If you've ever made chocolates using a double boiler you know exactly what I'm talking about.

6. Once the wax is melted and is at the specified temperature, add your dyes and scents if you wish. You'll notice though that adding these items (and your first time making a candle you might want to forego these) lowers the temperature of the wax.

Before you can go to the next step, you'll need to bring your wax up to the desired temperature range of between 120 to 150 degrees Farhenheit.

7. Once the melted wax has reached this temperature range, you may safely remove the top section of the double boiler from its bottom mate. As you do this, carefully pay attention to the steam that will be coming from the boiling water as well as any water which may be dripping from the bottom of the top section of your pot.

Congratulations! You've successfully melted the wax contents for your first candle. You're feeling proud of yourself, looking down at the liquid wax. But now, what do you do with it?

This is where your pouring pot comes into play.

8. Pour the melted wax from the double boiler into a

pouring pot. Using a pouring pot is recommended for two reasons. It greatly reduces the chances of spilling melted wax. And it makes filling the molds or containers easier and safer.

This step is not required when you pour large amounts of wax into another container.

Do not overfill the pour pot. In fact, don't fill the pouring pot more than 70% full. Once you've completed this, replace the top section of the double boiler on top of its mate.

Once you have the melted wax safely into the pouring pot, you're ready to pour it into the mold itself.

Before you do that though, there are three very important safety tips of which you should be aware:

•   **Pour slowly.** Now is not the time to rush through your project. Pour carefully.

•   **If you should spill the melted wax, clean up the spill as soon as possible -- immediately if at all possible.**

•   **Wipe off all wax drippings on the side of the double boiler or the pouring pot immediately.**

Before pouring your wax from the pouring pot to the container of your choice, you need to prepare your mold in two different ways.

8. You may want to spray mold release into the structure to facilitate the eventual removal of the hardened candle from it. You can substitute vegetable oil for the mold release spray, it works just as well. Be careful, though because you don't want to use much.

A little vegetable oil goes a long, long way!

9. Next, "set" the wick of the candle. Otherwise, you'll not have a way to burn your new creation (Of course, you might not want to burn it for a while, just sit back and admire it!).

Several ways exist for setting wicks, I'm going to show you the easiest for now and one of the most versatile ways. Make sure you use a wick that has a metal tab. Place this into your mold with the metal tab in the center of the mold.

10. Anchor the wick by taping its top to a pencil placed across the mold's opening.

Now you're ready for the final touch, actually filling your mold with the melted wax. You're beginning to see why it's important to have your work space prepared ahead of time. You'll also want to have your mold sprayed and the wick set in your mold prior to starting as well.

11. Now, that your wax is at the proper temperature (no hotter than 160 degrees F.) carefully fill the container to your desired level. Don't use all of the wax in the pouring pot at this point. You will need it again before you remove your candle from the mold (Be patient! You'll see what I'm talking about in just a moment!) So just use about 80 percent of it for now.

12. Allow your wax to completely cool. With experience, you'll be able to judge the time. For now, you'll want to give it at least six hours, depending on the size of your candle.

This is not a step you can rush, so don't even try. The

slow-cooling process provides the best results. As you read more, you'll discover some individuals suggest that you speed the cooling process by placing the candle in the refrigerator or even the freezer. This really isn't a good idea.

I'll only place my candles in the refrigerator when they refuse to budge out of a mold and I've tried just about every other trick I can think of. But it's best not to get into the habit of immediately placing candles in the fridge.

Once your candle has cooled completely, you may be disappointed. You probably have already noticed that the wax has sunken in slightly in the middle of the structure. Don't worry about this, this is a normal occurrence.

And it's exactly why you saved some of your wax. Now is the time you melt it back down, bringing it to a temperature of 185 degrees F. this time. During a second melting session, you can take the wax to a higher temperature. It increases the adhesion among the various layers of wax.

13. Re-pour your melted wax into the candle to a level that just barely covers the wax from the first pouring. When you do this, you're effectively hiding any "seam lines." Now, allow the candle to cool completely again.

14. Once your candle has completely cooled, remove the pencil from the wick.
15. Trim the wick so its about one-quarter of an inch long.

Your final step: Enjoy your very personalized creation!

One Step Beyond "The Basics": Additives and More

Congratulations! You've finished your first project. It was, indeed, a good feeling to make that candle. And if you made it with your children, all of you, no doubt, had a great time doing it. In fact, if you enjoyed that experience with your children, you can rightly claim you made more than just a candle: you created memories for them.

As you create more candles (and memories), you'll discover times that your instructions for a specific project may require more than just pouring wax into a mold. You may be required to use certain additives, or luster crystals or even snow wax. These are just a few of the variations you'll enjoy as you journey through this hobby.

While these aren't entirely essential at the moment to your enjoyment or enhancement of the candle making hobbies, they certainly are items you might want to familiarize yourself with. Let's do it now, so the next time your talking "candle making" with someone, you won't be totally lost if she speaks of one of these times.

Additives

As you make various types of candles, you may discover that some additives to your basic wax are necessary. This is especially true when you work with paraffin wax. As you get more experience, you'll know whether you need to add certain substances to keep your project from being damaged by the sun. Or you may need to include an additive to make the candle opaque. The following are just a few you may eventually use.

Luster Crystals

These gorgeous crystals provide a brilliant sheen and an opaqueness to your project. Luster crystals also give your candle a longer burning time. For best results, you'll want to *use one teaspoon of luster crystals for every two pounds of wax*. The crystals need to be melted first, before they are placed in the melted wax.

Microcrystalline wax

The presence of microcystalline wax creates a harder candle. To obtain the best results of this additive, you'll want to *use two tablespoons of these this wax to a pound of your base wax*. Like the luster crystals, microcrystalline wax needs to be melted separately, then poured into the melted paraffin for you to notice the best results.

Snow wax

This particular additive enhances the opaqueness of the candle, while giving it a high luster. It also prevents that "hot weather" sag that affects so many candles. But snow wax also performs several other vital jobs as well, including increasing the burning time of your candle and improving its texture.

For these two reasons alone, you may want to learn more about this additive. For best results, use only *one teaspoon of snow wax for every one pound of wax you use.*

Stearin

This specific additive improves the candle's burning time as well as provides opacity or a white appearance to your project. When you decide to your hand at this, you should use *only two teaspoons for every pound of wax.*

Vybar

This strange-sounding additive hardens the candle and reduces the shrinkage of the wax. For optimum results, use one teaspoon of vybar for every pound of paraffin wax you use. Vybar also affects your candle by giving it a opacity. If you don't want that opaque look to your candle, be careful how much of this you use.

Help! I think I made a mistake! Troubleshooting Your Creations

This is the common cry of the novice candle-making. And I certainly should know. I've been the person crying that phrase more than once. In fact, I can't tell you how many candles I refused to give away and actually threw away because I thought they were ruined.

Had I known some of the secrets of salvaging a candle that I share with you, I would not only have save myself much distress, but quite a few candles as well.

As with any hobby or adventure, you're bound to make a few bumps in the road during your first couple of forays into the field. Or, you may encounter some strange phenomenon that has never occurred before.

It totally throws you off guard. And of course, since you've never seen it before you haven't a clue how to fix it -- or even if your candle can be "fixed."

Let me tell you, there are few mistakes in candle making that cant be repaired. And here are just a few of the ways you can spot your less than perfect candles and make them shine, not only in your family's eyes, but in yours as well.

Help! The candle sticks to the mold!

This is one of the biggest problems of the new candle maker. The first step in repairing this situation is to do nothing. That's right do nothing! Well, you could busy yourself around the kitchen or munch on that bag of potato chips that's calling your name.

Why? Because at least 98 percent of the time, this particular problem remedies itself. If your candle won't separate from the mold, it just might not be cool enough to be removed. Add another 15 minutes to your cooling time. Try removing the candle from the mold then.

If you still have no luck, try letting it cool for yet another 15 minutes. Go along. Do something else for now. Allow Mother Nature, in the form of cooling the candle, run its course.

If, after the second 15-minute respite, you still can't remove the mold, then simply pop your candle into the freezer for 10-minute intervals. This is not the ideal solution, but when nothing else works, it's at least a way to save a mold and a candle (because right about now, if you're anything like me, you're ready to throw both either in the waste basket or across the room in anger. Not that I recommend doing either mind you. Nor have I actually done either, honest!)

Remember though this problem may be solved by adding just a little more silicone spray or releasing agent with your next group of candles. Apply the releasing agents to the inside of the mold prior to actually pouring any wax.

Clean mold?

Sometimes candles stick to molds despite all the advice above simply because they haven't been cleaned thoroughly after their last use. This should help any future sticking problems. You just need to be careful cleaning these supplies. Clean the inside of the mold but don't scratch the inside surface. Any scratches made on the inside of this mold will show up as "designs" on the candle itself.

Help! I have a stray wax drip along the side of my candle!

Why of course there's wax on the side of your candle. It's made of wax. But I understand exactly what you're talking about. There seems to be a protrusion of wax along the outside surface of your candle that's keeping it from feeling and looking smooth. How in the world did that happen?

Remember your second pouring of wax? You may have overfilled that small indentation. It's easy enough to do. The excess wax just simply slid down the inside of your mold. And since the fast majority of the candle was dry at this point, you know have a secondary "wax drip" as it were.

There's not a lot you can do to fix the problem without getting into the "noticeable repair zone," But at least knowing what caused it can help you avoid it in the future.

You'll have to keep that particular candle for your own enjoyment. And if any person does points out this flaw, simply tell them it's part of the unique design and it took a lot of talent to craft that drip to look perfect.

Help! The surface of my candle is pitted!

Again this is a problem that, unfortunately cannot be fixed with that particular candle (what a pity, you must keep that one for yourself, too!), but can be easily remedied with the next candles you pour.

A pitted surface indicates that the wax was too cool by the time you poured it. Now, all you need to do with this particular problem is decide where in the process the cooling occurred. Did you not heat the wax to a sufficient temperature?

If you suspect this, then just make sure that you get the temperature to the highest, safest range for the type of wax you're using.

Did it cool too quickly in your pouring pot? If it did, then you need to re-think the order in which you produce your candles. What can you do differently that prepares your quicker for pouring?

Help! My gel candle has too many air bubbles!

This is a common problem. Of course, many individual candle-making pour their gel wax intentionally to create bubbles. They consider them a integral part of the candle.

But if you have bubbles where you think you shouldn't, then just use a different pouring technique. The air bubbles usually occur when you pour the gel wax straight into the container.

Next time you pour your gel, think of it as pouring a stein of beer -- even if you'e never poured a beer in your life. An experienced bartender pouring beer tries pour so very little foam forms at the top of the glass.

He accomplishes this by holding the stein or glass at a slight angle and allows the beer itself to hit the side of glass. While you don't exactly want to hold the container at an angle, you do want to pour your gel as close to the side of the container as possible. As you get more experienced in pouring, you'll get better at this. In the meantime, if any person dare mention it, you can always say it's part of the creative process!

Help! My candle isn't burning properly!

This is a common problem, especially among those individuals just learning. It's difficult sometimes to judge the size of the wick needed for candles. Of course, guides exist, but sometimes you just can't decide. And sometimes when you finally do decide, your decision . . . well, let's just say it's less than ideal. Yes, I've had my share of less than idea choices in wicks as well. (How do you think I became such a great troubleshooter?)

Is the flame of your candle glowing unusually large for the size of your candle? If so, then it indicates that the wick you chose is too large for the project. Or it could just mean that you didn't trim the end of it off short enough.

Start with trimming the end to about a quarter of a inch above the wax. See is this doesn't help. If it doesn't then the next time you make this size candle, just use a smaller wick.

If your flame isn't burning strong enough, then you probably have a wick that's too small. The next time you make this size candle, increase the size of your wick.

And if your wick won't light at all, it's most likely you forgot to prime it -- giving it that nice soaking in hot wax.

Help! My multi-colored candle contains white lines!

Hmm? Didn't count on those white lines where two colors meet? Nor should you. Those lines really shouldn't be there. In all probability, the temperature of the second wax was too low when you poured it.

Review your steps to see where the problem may lie. Then try to remedy it for the next multiple color candle you make!

Help! My candle spits at me when it's lit!

No, a candle spitting at you doesn't mean it hates you. (Aren't we getting a bit touchy here?)

Now I have a question for you. Were making a candle in which you're using ice in some way. Wax tends to hiss when you make "ice candles" or the "fire and ice" candles I'll be showing you in a following chapter. The hissing sound simple indicates that some water has become trapped inside the wax.

If this becomes an overwhelming problem, simply blow the flame out. Then, you'll want to carefully tip the candle at an angle to drain off the rest of the water that may be present. That should end your candle's imitation of a snake!

Help! My wax is hissing and bubbling in the double boiler!

From time to time this is a problem you may encounter. As you carefully heat the wax it indeed may hiss or even bubble. This simply means your wax contains some impurities.

If your wax does indeed contain impurities, please let the manufacturer of the wax know this. You may even want to keep your packaging. If other wax from the same company also hisses and bubbles, you may eventually want to change suppliers.

This may also mean that some water has gotten into the wax. Be sure that the heat on your double boiler isn't turned too high. If the heat is too high, it could mean the water in the lower level is boiling and splashing into the wax.

CHAPTER 5:
Making Candles

Have you made your first candle yet? If you have, then I'm quite sure you've caught the flavor . . . fun . . . and fantasy of candle making. No doubt your first creation was successful. Did your family "ooh" and "ahh" over it?

And now you've turn to this chapter because you're ready to continue on to more creative projects. Oh yes, I can see you're a candle maker for life, now!

The All-Purpose Container Candle

The name container candle says it all. But if you need some type of explanation of just exactly what one looks like, think about those candles you've seen in square glass jars, or canning jars, or any open topped container. You'll actually burn the candle in the container in which you're making it.

This is probably one of the easiest -- and the most popular -- type of candle to make. Before you get yourself all ready to make this, notice that I've added a small piece of "equipment" to your candle making needs.

I haven't mentioned this before, but it's a little secret that you might want to adopt when making this type of candle. I'm going to have you tear apart a perfectly good pen -- the inexpensive "Bic" type. And you're going to use the outside plastic barrel to help guide the wick. You'll see exactly what I mean in the instructions below.

1. Prepare your wax.

Prepare your double boiler to melt your wax. As usual, you'll want to get your wax to a temperature of between 160 and 170 degrees F. Once the substance has melted completely, place any additive you've decided on. Mix these thoroughly. It's best to place these additives in the following order:

a. *vybar or stearic acid*
b. *fragrance oil*
c. *dye* This needs to be done as close to last as possible. Some people prefer to add the fragrance absolutely last. But many choose to add the dye last. This gives you a good visual confirmation that everything has mixed thoroughly.

While your wax is melting, you can perform the next several steps. Just make sure to check back on your wax periodically.

2. Add pre-tabbed wicks to your containers.

This is where the Bic pen comes in handy. Once you've taken apart your pen, keep only the round, hollow barrel of the pen.   Straighten your wicks, but don't worry, you need to be a perfectionist about it.

Insert one of the pre-tabbed wicks through the barrel of the pen. (Six inch wicks are actually the best for this) If you have a length of wick that is different from this, you may have to improvise a bit. You're actually going to be using the point of the barrel as a "handle which makes working with the wick easier.

Hold the wick within the barrel. Apply hot glue to the base of the wick tab. You may want to use either a glue pot or a hot-glue gun for this portion of the step.

Using the barrel as a guide for the wick, press the tab to the center of your container. Now, you can slide the barrel off the wick.

3. Secure the top of the wick.

Using either a pencil or a good quality clothespin, secure the top of your wick. Clothespins actually work quite well for container candles that have an opening up to three inches.

Doing this provides some support to keep the wick centered during the wax's cooling process.

4. Pre-heat your container.

When your wax is melted and ready, pre-heat your container. You can do this with a heat gun, but be careful here. The temperature of your wax as it gets poured into the container is about 150 degrees F. If you use a heat gun, you'll discover that the gun gets hotter than that.

This step is not actually vital but it does help improve your finished product. This helps you to pour the wax at a lower temperature without worrying about trapping bubbles. Pre-heating the container also helps improve the adhesion of the wax to the glass.

5. Pour your wax.

You'll want to pour your wax from your double boiler to your pouring pot. Then transfer the wax from the pouring pot into the container. Fill it to the level you want. If this particular container has a lid, remember to leave enough room so the lid will close.

You'll also want to save approximately 20 percent of the wax for later. But do not return this wax to the heat source.

Allow the wax to cool completely. Typically this takes about six hours. But, there's absolutely nothing wrong with allowing your wax to dry overnight. Remember that the slower your wax cools, the better it will melt. This is especially so when it comes to container candles. Don't be in a hurry and, above all, try not to rush the cooling process ("We will cool no candle before its time" should become your new mantra!)

Once your candle has cooled completely, you'll notice that the wax around the wick may have sunk in some. Don't worry. That's where the wax you saved comes in handy. Re-heat this wax to a temperature of approximately 185 degrees (on a second pour you can take the wax to a slightly higher temperature safely). This higher temperature also helps to reduce any visible seams between the now two layers of wax you're making.

You'll re-pour this wax to a level that just barely covers the wax from the first pour. This too will help camouflage any seam lines. Now, once again allow your candle to cool.

6. Trim the wick.

Once the candle has completely cooled, you can remove the clothespin that has been holding the wick. Trim the wick to about a quarter inch of the wax.

And now for the tough part: Enjoy it!

Making Molded Pillar Candles

So you think you know what a pillar candle is? Well, when I first began making candles, so did I. And then I realized how wrong I was. But it was more own fault. I just "assumed" from the name that any tall candle was a "pillar" candle.

How wrong I was!

Pillar candles come in a wide variety of shapes, from conical, to cubical to a star-like shape and even a pyramid shape. The distinguishing characteristic of this type of candle is not so much the shape, but the mold which houses the candle.

The molds are made from sheet metal, aluminum or sometimes less commonly plastic, latex or silicone. When you purchase your mold, you'll notice immediately that the largest variety of molds can be found in the sheet metal category. These molds also come with a mold screw which you use to ensure the wick stays in place.

The pillar candle is, in fact, one of the most popular types of candles to make.

The instructions I provide below have been created specially for a pillar candle made from sheet metal. Should you have a mold made from another substance, check to see if there are any accompanying instructions. If there are, then follow the manufacturer's instructions.,

Here's what you'll need to make a pillar candle:

- Wax
- Additives -- wax or scent
- Metal pillar mold
- Wich
- Wick screw
- Wick rod (a wooden skewer works well)
- Mold sealer putty

1. Prepare your work place with everything you'll need.

Yes, I know you're getting to be an old pro at this. If you have any doubts go back to Chapter Four and review the more detailed steps I've provided there.

2. Melt your wax

While your wax is melting, you should be able to review these instructions again and get the other equipment, tools and supplies ready for use.

3. Place the wick through the wick hole

Thread a wick through the wick-hole in the base of your mold. Sometimes individuals complain they have problems getting the wick to go through the hole. Usually this occurs because the wick has become frayed. If you find you're encountering this problem, then dip the end of the wick into some molten wax. Roll the wick through your fingers, forming a nice pointed end.

4. Secure the wick to the wick rod.

Keep the wick within the hole, tie one end of it to the wick rod. If you don't have a wick rod, many home candle makers use a pencil or even a wooden skewer used for cooking "kabobs."

5. Secure the wick to the wick hole.

Next, you're going to make sure that you've secured the wick to the wick hole. For this step you'll need a Phillips screwdriver for the wick screw. Be careful not to tighten the wick screw too much. It may cut the wick or even damage your mold.

The purpose of this screw is just to keep the wick from sliding back through the hole. Some people mistakenly believe it is to actually seal the hole. Your wick should be taut. But don't make it too tight. In my enthusiasm as a novice candle maker I tightened this too much, and I warped the mold itself. So once again you can learn from my stupid mistakes.

Trim the wick. You'll only want about one-half to one inch of wick.

6. Seal the wick hole.

Using the mold sealer, seal the wick hole, the wick screw, and yes the wick itself. You're doing all of this to prevent any leakage of the molten wax. You'll press the sealer firmly into place, ensuring a tight seal. You may want to take the extra precaution of lightly wrapping the wick around the screw itself before applying the sealer. The idea is that you don't want any of the wick showing.

7. Initial pour

It may seem as if it took a long time for us to get to this

point, but now you can perform your initial pour. For pillar candles you want to ensure that the temperature of your melted wax is between 175 and 185 degrees Fahrenheit.

It's at this point that you may also include any additives -- like fragrance of dye. Add these into the pot, mix well. Pour the wax into your pouring pot and then into the mold.

You also need to act as a "Boy Scout" as you pour into the mold. Don't be surprised if you acquire one or more small leaks. Deal with these quickly simply by having towels or paper towels ready to sop up the wax spill.

You'll want to fill your molds to approximately one-half inch from the top. Be sure that you leave enough wax in the pouring pot for the second pour. And as usual, don't place this reserve wax back to the heat source just yet.

8. Create relief holes.

After you've allowed your candle to cool for a short period, you'll notice that a surface has formed on your wax. You'll want to poke what is known as relief holes into the base of the candle. These holes help to accommodate the natural shrinkage which occurs as the wax hardens.

Position the holes around the wick and make them about one inch in depth. Specifically, the relief holes provide a ventilation system so the wax can suck air through in an attempt to compensate for the decreased volume.

If the candle did not have these holes, several adverse affects may occur. Without the holes, air cavities may develop, the wick may get pulled off-center or the external walls of the candle may become deformed.

Check on the candles several times during the cooling process. It very well could be that you need to re-open these holes as the wax hardens.

Allow the candle to cool completely before you move on to the next step. Don't rush the cooling process. It may take up to several hours. If the candle is very large it could take a day or more.

9. Re-pour

Once you're satisfied the candle is completely cool, re-melt the 20 percent of wax that you hold in reserve. As usual, the wax can be melted at a temperature that is approximately 5 to 10 degrees higher than the original melt. The higher temperature of the wax increases its ability to adhere to the different layers.

When your wax has reached the desired temperature, pour the melted wax into the sink holes you've created. Fill these holes just below the level of the first filing. If you fill these holes any higher, you may cause a visible horizontal seam line on the exterior of the finished candle. Overfilling may also cause the wax to seep between the mold and the candle. This would affect the attractiveness of the finish.

Allow the candle to completely cool before you go on to the next step.

10. Remove the candle from the mold.

Remove the mold sealer and the wick screw. The candle should slide easily out of the mold if it's completely cooled. If the candle doesn't slide out with ease, place the candle and mold in the refrigerator for about 15 minutes. Then try to take the candle out of the mold again. The intentional cool period in the refrigerator helps to shrink the wax even more. That, in turn helps the wax to separate from the mold itself.

The end of the candle attached to the wick-rod is the bottom of the candle. Trim the wick -- flush with the base of the candle -- at this end.

Some individuals take the time at this point of the process to also level the base of the candle. They place the candle on a cookie sheet sitting on top of a pot of boiling water. You'll use this heated cookie sheet to help to melt some of the wax until the candle's base is completely flat.

Now, you can trim the wick at the other end of the candle to about one-quarter of an inch.

Congratulations, you've created your first pillar candle.

Making votive candles

You've seen them, even if you haven't called them by their proper names -- the small candles you love to burn in individualized holders. These candles are about an inch and a half in diameter and no more than several inches tall. When my daughter was younger, she used to ask me to make those "baby candles." I'm not sure if she really thought they would grow up to be adult candles one day!

These are, of course, votive candles. These are most recognized with several types of religious rituals. Indeed, the candle -- all sizes and shapes -- holds deep symbolism within the church, especially the Catholic Church. A large white candle, referred to as the Pascal candle represents Christ -- the true Light. The smaller candles are symbols of each of us who attempts to become Christ like.

The votive candle has its own history. Its origins can be found in the Old Testament practice of sacrifice. The candle was scented; the fragrance sent upward toward the heavens represented prayer. The burning of the votive candle itself represented a person's sacrifice.

Today, many individuals light a candle before a statue. This is said to be symbolic of a person's love for God. According to some, the simple lighting of a votive candle, represents a person's desire to dedicate himself to a higher power.

Most of us don't hold such lofty ideals as we light these delightful candles. We just know that they emit a gloriously comforting light, whose flame, if the air currents are just right, dance magically and beautifully.

If you're like me, you've bought literally dozens -- or more -- of these candles in your lifetime. Now here's your chance to make your own!

1. Prepare the wax.

As usual, begin to set up your double boiler and ready all the supplies to melt your wax. Prepare any additives

-- scents or dyes -- that you may wish to add. For the votive candle, you'll want your candle wax to reach a melting temperature of approximately 175 degrees F.

Remember not to put in any additives until your wax is completely melted.

Even before you pour your wax, consider coating the molds lightly with a very thin film of a mold-release agent. Spray a silicone coating agent or even a vegetable oil cooking product inside the molds. The purpose of this is the aid in the release of the finished candle from the mold.

2. The first pour

Take your votive molds and place them on a newspaper-lined surface. Since these molds are smaller than most, sometimes accidents happen. (At least it always did when I was in charge of pouring. My aim with the smaller molds never seemed to be quite as accurate as it should.)

Fill each mold to its lip. The goal (which seems obvious, I know!) is to fill the molds without over-filling them. If you choose to pour the wax to any level lower than the lip, the final product may have a visible, noticeable and unattractive seam line when the project is completed. While pouring, try to take care to minimize the number of bubbles that appear during the pouring process.

As usual, you'll want to save approximately 20 percent of the wax for the second re-pour. But you don't want to return it to the heat source just yet.

3. Add pre-tabbed wicks

You've noticed that we've changed the steps a little here. I haven't had you insert any wicks yet. No, it wasn't a mistake on my part. While the candles are cooling, take the wicks straighten them. At this point they don't need to be absolutely straight. Just get them as close to straight as possible.

Once the wax congeals some, you may insert your pre-tabbed wicks. The tab should naturally adhere to this material. Be careful exactly where you plant the tab. It should be as close to the center of the mold as possible.

It's a good idea to wait until the wax congeals to place your wick in the votive mold so it won't interfere with the ultimate firmness of the primed wick.

Supposedly, this is also the ideal temperature for the metal tab to stick to the base of the mold. If you attempt to place the wick when the wax possesses even a slightly higher temperature, it may be a little more difficult to make the placement.

I can see that waiting to place the wick makes you a bit nervous. Just trust me on this when you make your first votives. You'll see exactly what I mean. And don't worry. Once you've placed the tab into the base of the mold, you'll still be able to do some manipulation of it to ensure that the wick is as straight as possible.

In some instances you may actually want to wait a few moments to allow the tab to create an even stronger bond with the base of the mold before you straighten the wick.

The cooling of the wax may pull your wick off center somewhat. Should this occur, you really need not be too concerned. It's actually very easy to remedy. A simple light tug straightens the wick. Don't tug too much though because you don't want to pull the tab from the base completely.

Now that you've taken care of your wick, allow the candle to cool completely. For a votive-size candle this should take approximately three to four hours.

4. Re-pouring the wax.

As usual, once the wax has dried completely, you'll notice some shrinkage. You'll have that tell-tale sink hole that always need to be filled. And yes, by now you're an old pro at what you do next, now aren't you?

Melt down the saved wax from the original pour. And you also know that you can melt to a slightly higher temperature than the first pour - approximately 10 to 15 degrees higher.

You probably, by this point, even know why you can do this. Yep! The higher temperature increases the adhesion of the layers.

Once you've re-poured, allowed the candles to cool once more.

5. Remove the votive candle from the mold.

Once you're sure the votive candles are completely cooled, take them from the mold. They normally will slide right out without any trouble. If you discover that your votives stubbornly cling to the mold, try freezing them for about five minutes. This usually cools them sufficiently to slide out.

If for some reason, even after this chill period, they

remain stubbornly in the mold, put them back into the freezer for a second five-minute period.

Sometimes even the best of candles are stubborn even after several stays in the 'deep freeze'. Some people find it helps to gently press the sides of the mold inward as you roll the mold in the palms of your hands. See if this doesn't work for you!

Making Tealight Candles

You've seen them, you've probably even bought them. And you or someone you know has undoubtedly fussed over these "cute little candles." Okay, so before I encountered my candle making hobby, I wasn't sure of their name. Now, I know these adorable little things are called tealight candles.

Today, you can even find a variety of gorgeous holders created especially for tealight candles.

Here's what you'll need to create your own, highly delightful, tealights:

- Votive or pillar wax
- Aluminum cup
- Tealight mold
- Wicks

1. Start out by laying the tealight molds on a flat, level surface. Insert what's called a votive pin in the mold. This particular piece of equipment helps to keep your wick straight. Spray a light coating of mold release or vegetable oil spray over the entire mold.

2. Prepare your wax. Prepare any color or fragrance you may want to include in your tealights.

3. Once the wax reaches the optimum temperature (again, about 175 degrees), pour the wax into the pouring pot.

4. And then pour the wax from the pouring pot into the tealight molds themselves. You'll notice that this specific mold has a lip that holds overflow wax.

5. Remove the pins and pop the tea lights out the molds. Using your fingers, clean any rough edges.

6. Now insert a pre-assembled wick assembly for tealights into the hold in the candle. Place this all into a tea light cup. You'll notice that the tealight cups have a small circular indentation at the bottom of about 15 mm. This is designed specifically to match tea light wicks.

Making Hand-Dipped -- or Taper -- Candles

Think Colonial Williamsburg. Your first thought is inevitably hand-dipped candles. These candles are probably the most unique you'll make, as they require you to dip the wicks directly into the wax, no transfer or pouring of wax is required. You'll see what I mean in a moment.

Another unique aspect of making dipping candles is that you'll be making these delectable lights two at a time. I'll show you exactly how that works in a few moments.

Give these candles a try and I guarantee that you'll be making them over and over again. Here's what you'll need to become the diva of hand-dipped candles:

- Paraffin wax (you'll probably want to start with approximately a half pound.
- Wooden spoon on which to hang your string
- Bowl for the cold water bath
- Candle Thermometer
- Wick.
- Dipping pot

How to choose a wick for a hand-dipped candle

Now would be the perfect time to clue you in with some insight on choosing the wick for hand-dipped candles. You're already keenly aware that wicks come in varying sizes. And you've probably noticed through your travels of your favorite local craft stores and the virtual candle making stores on the internet that they tend to increase in size in half-inch increments.

You'll want to match the size of the wick to the estimated size of your candle on a one on one ratio. What do I mean by this? You'll want to use a half-inch wick for a hand-dipped candle that's going to be an estimated half inch. And if your candle plans are to create one-inch candles, then you'll want to purchase one-inch wicks.

Yes, it really is that simple -- at least in this particular case!

1. Prepare you wax.

In this process, you may even want to give some thought to cutting your wax into small pieces. It melts quicker this way. Begin melting. Remember to use your thermometer to test the temperature. With a dipped candle, you need a temperature of about 160 degrees.

You'll also want to wait until the wax is completely melted before adding any scent or color to the molten wax.

2. Prepare your dipping pot.

If your melting pot in your double boiler isn't wide or deep enough to deep candles in (about 12 inches) then you'll want to bring out the dipping pot we spoke about in an earlier chapter. You'll pour your wax from the double boiler into the pouring pot. It's from here that you get to perform the 'creative' portion of the candle-making process.

3. Prepare your wicks

Your next step is to cut the wick to the desired length of your candles -- plus a little extra to hold. Here is a good rule of thumb to follow -- especially if you're starting out. If you are making two 10-inch candles cut about 23 inches of wick.

4. Dip your wicks

Now, you're just about to start the fun part: the actual dipping of the candles. First, you'll be making the candles two at a time, so keep this in mind as you read these instructions. Double the wick over your finger.

Dip the wick in the wax for a few seconds. Lift it back out. Now allow the wax to cool for a minute or so. You'll want a minute or so of "cooling time" between each dipping period.

Initially, you may find this a little difficult. At first the wick, which doesn't weigh much will want to float on top of the wax. As you continue dipping this ceases to be an issue.

5. Continue the dipping process

Repeat the dipping process until the candles have reached the desired thickness. If lumps appear on the surface of the candle, simply roll the warm candles on a smooth surface. This should smooth out the candle itself.

6. The cooling process

Once these candles are as thick as you'd like them, allow them to cool. The best way to cool them is to hang them in a place where they will be undisturbed.

7. Trimming your candles

Once dry, you'll want to use a sharp knife to trim the bottom of the candle in order to remove any excess wax. Trimming also helps to create a straigh⁻ edge at the bottom of the candles so they'll stand up well.

8. Hang to dry more

Allow the candles to dry completely. Only then should you cut the wicks.

Once cut, you can enjoy them or give them as gifts for your friends and family to enjoy.

Let's Make Gel Candles

Are you ready to venture into the craft of making gel candles? Good! These unique creations are the hottest variety on the market today (pun definitely intended, sorry!). And with good reason. One look at these candles and you know they are not your grandmother's candle.

They take all the beauty, glory and comfort of the candle and knock it up one Emeril Lagasse notch: BAM!

Clear . . . or translucent . . . or filled with color. These gel candles can actually hold a variety of decorative accessories inside the gel itself. And that means unlimited potential for your imagination.

Gel candles have a unique rubbery texture to them which actually glow when the candle is lit. Your company will rave about your unique creations. Should you decide to part with any of them to give them as gifts, the recipients of these candles will marvel over them!

Let's get started with the very basics of gel candle making. Then I'm going to let you and your imagination take it from there!

In some very basic ways, making gel candles is no different than making a paraffin-based candle. You melt your wax -- in this case gel wax --, add the color and fragrance, pour into a pouring pot, then a pre-wicked container, then you cool, trim your wick and viola! You have a delightful gel candle.

The difference occurs, as you'll see, when you discover the temperature at which the gel wax can be taken (so be extremely careful when working with it!). But that's not all. You'll also thoroughly enjoy (now that's an understatement!) how easy it is to ad one more step to the process. And that is to include, in the hot wax any embedded accessories that you care to.

What are we waiting for? Let's get started!

Here's what you'll need:

- Gel wax
- Thermometer
- Stirring utensil (not wood this time)
- Metal skewer (if you use embeds, you'll move them around with this)
- Potato peeler (Yes! You'll use this to shave off small slivers of block dye)
- Toothpicks (This is necessary to add the liquid dye to the gel)
- Wax paper (For use in checking the gel color)
- Containers (To hold the final product!)

Before we even talk about the process, let's talk a little about the type of container you'll want to put your gel candle in. Since they are so clear, you'll want to be able to see through the container into the beauty of the candle itself.

That means you'll want a clear container. And you already know you don't want to use plastic (especially with the heat of a gel candle) which may melt. You'll want to avoid the thinner glass containers though for this project. With the high temperature of a burning gel candle, the thinner glass may crack.

The gel

Candle gel can be found in just about any quality craft store. If you can't find it locally, you can definitely purchase it online. When you're trying to decide how much wax you'll need for a particular project, simply begin by measuring the amount of water required to fill your selected containers. This is the amount of gel you'll need as well. And gel wax is actually reusable, so don't worry if you overestimate the amount you need. You can always use it on later projects.

Dyes

Many individuals who are avid gel makers swear by the dyes created especially for gel candles. And feel free to buy these at your local candle store. But you might be pleased to know -- whether you're working from a budget or just don't want to invest in the specialty dye -- that the dyes for paraffin candles work just as well.

And it very well could be that for your first foray into this amazing adventure, you'll just want to use those!

Fragrances

Unlike the dyes, you can't use fragrances for paraffin-based candles. Those scents that aren't specifically created for the gel candle may, once you place them in the melted gel, cloud your finished product. They may ultimately create a fire hazard by lowering the flashpoint of the gel.

Wicks

Gel candles really need zinc-cored wicks. They are stiffer than the wicks for the other waxes so they stay straight in the gel. These specialty wicks are available with or without anchors -- or tabs.

And before you even place your wick in the wax, you'll want to be sure that they're pre-treated to avoid bubbling.

1. Melt the gel

Ahh! Here's one of the very significant differences between gel wax and other waxes. I've already mentioned that gel wax needs a higher temperature in order to melt.

Well, let's dig into this difference just a little more before you begin to melt your gel. You're going to notice right off that gel doesn't melt in the traditional sense.

Gel just gets hotter when you place it on the burner. As a result, it thins slowly. Then as it cools, it thickens, gradually. Constantly keep this in mind. You're going to look at this gel and realize it doesn't change "form" in quite the same way your paraffin does.

The maximum temperature you should take gel wax too is 220 degrees. It gets to its thinnest consistency when it hits the temperature of 180 degrees. You can safely take the gel to 220 degrees. **But no hotter.**

I know that up to this point, I've lectured you about the very real need of a double boiler. This is the one wax that defies that need. Because it needs more heat to become pliable, flexible and well, gel-like, you need to be the gel wax over a direct heat source. But that also means you monitor the wax constantly.

You may also want to consider cutting your gel into smaller pieces so the "melting" occurs a little faster.

2. Place a bit of hot glue in the center of the container bottom in which you're planning on pouring the gel. Securely place the wick in it. Allow the glue some time to set.

3. If you want to add color to your gel, do so once the your mixture had reached 200 degrees. Add just a little at a time. You can always add more dye if the color is quite right; you can't take the dye out!

4. Add any fragrance. Most individuals sue about one-third of a teaspoon for every glass of melted gel. If you'd like a stronger scent, then add a little moe than this.

5. Pre-heat the container in which you're going to pour your gel wax in the oven. You want it to be no hotter than 160 degrees. This reduces the presence of bubbles.

6. If you're placing embedding material into your work of art, then dip them in the hot gel first. Then arrange them in the pre-heated container. When arranging your accessories, it's best to keep them as close to the sides of the container as possible. In this way, they are easier to enjoy.

7. Pour the gel into the container. Place the container on a level surface. Pour the gel slowly and carefully down the side.

8. Straighten the wick. Roll it on a pencil to keep it upright and straight.
9. Allow the candle time to cool.

10. Trim the wick to about one-quarter inch.

> **How far that little candle throws its beams!**
> **So shines a good dead in a naughty world.**
> William Shakespeare

Making Beeswax Candles

With this type of wax, you have a choice. You can melt it and follow the instructions you used for the paraffin wax candles, or you can do some quick and easy "rolling" and create beautiful candles without actually melting your beeswax.

While you may not think this is very exciting, a younger member of your family may this is . . . well, the "bees knees" that she or he can make beautiful candles just about all by himself.

Here's how to make "rolled candles" from beeswax!

These are the supplies you'll need:

- Sheets of beeswax. These come in the dimension of 8 inch by 16 inch sheets
- Wicked primed for beeswax and a one-inch candle
- A matte knife, sharp knife or a razor blade (Sometimes I just pull out a kitchen paring knife if I can't find anything else.)
- A surface on which you can cut

1. Lay out your sheet of beeswax.

2. Cut the wick to about three-quarter of an inch longer than the sheet of wax is long.

3. Carefully lay the wick along the edge of the sheet.

4. Begin rolling the sheet by carefully bending over about one-eighth of the wax.

5. Enclose the wick within this small channel. Work from one end of the candle to the other. Press firmly to make sure the wax fits tightly around the wick. (This is the *only time* I'll ever tell you to "press hard" with these sheets.

6. Continue to roll, very slowly and very straight. From here on out, you're handling these sheets very gently and very carefully. You don't want to either compress or warp the honeycomb pattern on the wax. Make sure both ends of the candle are straight.

7. Roll until you get to the end of the sheet.

8. Add another sheet, if desired. Align this second sheet up to the edge of your first beeswax sheet. Use your thumb or thumbnail to press these two sheets together, then roll.

9. Add as many sheets as you have planned.

10. Trim the wick.

There you have it. You have a great idea of some of the different types of candles available to you. Armed with these instructions, you're definitely well equipped to continue your candle making interests for a while.

For every type of candle I've presented, you're limited in the decorations, colors and scents of these candles only by the limits of your own imagination. Yes, you've made container candles, but each one can be one-of-a-kind creations.

After you've made a few, you may be wondering just how many candles your house can hold. If you're like me, you've got candles on your book shelves . . . candles on your kitchen counter . . . candles on your bedstand . . . candles just about everywhere.

CHAPTER 6:
Candles as Gift Ideas

Candles are synonymous with warmth, love and harmony.

So what better gift to give the next time you're invited to a party, a picnic or even just for an evening of friendship.

As a full-fledge candle maker now, you're probably searching for "excuses" to make candles. I'm betting right about now, every time you haul out your wax and other candle making paraphernalia, your family probably just moans.

Ah! But you, on the other hand, enter the "Candle Making Zone." It's zen for the candle maker, as you become one with whatever project you're currently working on.

The perfect gift:
The fire and Ice candle

Here's a great idea for a candle. I call it the "Fire and Ice" candle -- when you see the final effect in person (or would that be "in candle") I'm sure you'll agree. You'll use crushed ice in the candle mold itself to achieve an effect three-dimensional effect in the wax itself.

The ice actually makes holes in the wax to create a stunningly beautiful effect. You'll make them initially to give away as gifts, but you'll be reluctant to give it away. So you'll just have to make a few extra!

Here's what you'll need to make this unique candle.

- Wax
- Metal candle mold
- Wick
- Mold sealer
- Pouring pitcher
- Double boiler
- Crushed ice
- Bucket or sink

1. Prepare your wick and your mold, including placing the wick screw and wick into place.

2. Crush ice cubes until they are approximately three-quarters of an inch. Spoon the ice into the mold itself until it is almost completely full. You'll want to leave some room just beneath the rim of your mold. This ensures that the wax has enough room to completely cover the ice.

3. During this time, you may begin melting your wax. When it's ready, transfer it from the double boiler to the pouring pot.

4. Now, you pour your wax over the ice in the mold. Instead of just pouring in one spot as you would normally do, try to move the pouring pot so your stream of molten wax is being poured evenly around the mold opening. You're doing this so the steady stream of wax in one spot does not melt a single hole through the ice.

All the wax to cool completely. Turn your mold upside down over a sink or your bucket. This releases the melted ice -- now reduced to ice water.

5. Remove the mold sealer and wick screw. Now, carefully remove the candle from the mold. Handle the finished candle carefully. It's quite fragile.

6. Trim the wick to its usual one-quarter inch. Allow the candle to dry at least one week before you light it. This gives the wick some time to dry. Attempting to light it before the wick is dry can cause a interruption in the continuity of the flame.

Make and Give
The Watermelon Candle

Want to give a great summertime candle? Why not fashion one to have the appearance of a watermelon -- the ultimate summertime treat!

Let's get started!

Here's what you'll need:

- Paraffin wax
- White Beeswax
- Pyramid mold
- Watermelon fragrance oil
- Black/Gray concentrated liquid dye
- Red/pink concentrated liquid dye
- Hunter green concentrated liquid dye
- 24-ply flat braid wick
- Mold sealer
- Cookie sheet

1. Heat about 2 ounces of beeswax in a double boiler. Add about two or three drops of black dye.

2. Pour several drops of the wax onto the cookie sheet. Allow this to dry slightly.

3. Peel the wax off the cookie sheet. Using your fingers, mold it into a teardrop shape. These "teardrops" will be your watermelon seeds. So feel free to make as many of these as you think you'll want in your piece of watermelon.

4. Press the warm "seeds" against the side of the pyramid mold. Keep pressing until they stick on their own. (They will; trust me on this one!)

5. Heat your paraffin wax in a double boiler. Add your fragrance. (You have several colors in this project, so you'll be doing several pours.) On your first pour, add five to seven drops of the red/pink liquid dye.

6. Prepare your mold with wick and mold sealer. Rest the mold on its square base.

7. Pour this first layer. Pour this layer when the temperature reaches approximately 145 degrees. This temperature is slightly lower than what we've been working with. This is called a "cold pour". This will enhance the "watermelon" appearance of the candle.

Leave about two inches of space from the edge of the mold.

8. Allow this to cool -- but not thoroughly. You don't want it to cool enough that it begins to separate from the mold. So you may want to keep a close eye on this.

9. Prepare the wax for the second pour.

10. Pour your second layer. This layer is white and it'll be about three-quarter of an inch in thickness. You'll want to wait until your wax is about 170 to 175 degrees before you pour this section.

11. Prepare your third pour. This is the green rind of your watermelon. You'll want to add about three drops of hunter green dye.

12. Pour this layer of wax. You'll want to pour this layer about 10 degrees hotter than you did the white layer. That means you'll want to get it to about 180 to 185 degree. And since this is the last pouring, be sure to save some wax for a repour.

13. Allow the candle to cool completely. Once the wax has completely cool, reheat the unused portion of the wax and fill in the sunken sections, as you usually do.

14. Carefully remove the candle from the mold. But don't do this until you're absolutely sure that the candle is completely cooled. If you like, take a heat gun and very gently blow it on the sides of the candle. This darkens the colors. It also creates small drops of wax to make it look more like a juicy slice of watermelon.

And there you have it! A watermelon candle perfect for a hostess gift for a summer party!

Canning jar candles

A candle gift that never gets old (even though it looks very old-fashioned) is the "canning jar" candle. You can easily make these container candles simply by using old canning jars you have around the house.

Don't have canning jars? Don't worry. If you spend any

time at flea markets or frequent garage sales, you'll find these. And if for some strange reason you can't, you can usually buy a dozen of these jars relatively cheaply at just about any grocery store or even some of the discount or "dollar" stores.

You simply use these jars as the containers. Then you follow the directions for the container candles. If you use paraffin wax, you can add any type of scent you'd like -- or think the recipient of your gift would like -- and the color that you'd like.

Some canning jars have embossed or raised decorations on the surface. Others are quite plain. Consider using plain jars as gel candles -- and then you can place all types of accessories in the jar! You can even top the jars off -- gel wax or otherwise -- with the lid of the canning jar.

For an added effect, you may want to wrap the lid in some type of gingham fabric to make give it more of a country look.

Candles are versatile gifts. They are every bit as appropriate as a Christmas present as a birthday present -- and every holiday in between. And since you love this hobby so much -- because let's face it, candle-making really is growing on you! -- you even try to think of holidays so you have a reason to give candles away.

It's not enough to give candles on Mother's Day, the Fourth of July, birthdays, New Year's Day, Easter, St. Patrick's Day, or even Valentine's Day. You keep looking for even more holidays. Well, Groundhog's Day may be pushing it a bit, now don't you think?

> # A candle loses nothing by lighting another candle.
> ## James Keller

If you know someone who is plagued by arthritis or other types of chronic pain, why not give her a candle scented specifically with aromatherapy scents. Lavender, for example, is used as a healing scent. Even if the candle doesn't actually relieve the person of her pain, she can at least bask the low glow of a homemade candle?

Here's an idea? If you're giving a candle to an elementary school teacher, why not embed crayons in the wax. You can make a gel candle or you can use a paraffin candle. Just add the crayons when the wax is not quite so hot. It could just possibly be the most original gift that she's ever been given.

Here's an idea for you. I bet you know at least one person who treats his pet pooch like a child. Why not make him a gel wax candle with some type of dog-related product inside. It could be anything from a Milk Bone treat to a small doggie toy. He'll get a kick out of it, and appreciate the thought. And who knows, maybe even Fido will enjoy the candle as well!

You can do the same thing with the crazy over-the-top cat lover in your life (you know the one, every one of us knows at least one of these!). Find something definitely feline that defines her relationship with her pet. Embed it into a gel wax candle -- and Presto! You have a gift that you can give at just about anytime!

CHAPTER 7:
Make a Wish and Blow Out A Candle:
Making Your Business Dreams Come True

It was the nineteenth century. Among the hundreds of thousands of immigrants who passed through Ellis Island seeking a better life in America were two Irish immigrants, William and James.

Oh, no! They didn't arrive together. They didn't even know the other existed at the time they landed in New York. But soon their paths crossed. James was a soap making by trade; William a candle maker.

Their paths crossed because these two gen-lemen married sisters. They became brothers-in-law.

As they settled into the United States, the land of opportunity, they looked at each other, wondering if they could make a go of their businesses in this country.

The year was 1837. Well, 20 years later they had their answer about whether they could succeed. In those first two decades they made their first million dollars. Their names: William Proctor and James Gomble.

Of course, the company's name is now synonymous not only with soap, but just about any health and beauty aid you can imagine: Procter & Gamble.

Of course, your candle making efforts will undoubtedly be more modest -- at least at the start. But, there is money to be made -- even today -- making candles. And if the truth be known (and don't tell too many people this because they'll all be planning to be your competition) there's quite a bit of money in candle making.

Consider this: seven out of every 10 households in this country burn candles. That means that 70 percent of us have some candles in the house. And that translates into the fact that 70 percent of the people you already know -- on average -- are your potential customers.

I'm not sure that there's another business out there that can boast those types of statistics. Okay, so we all have to eat!

It just depends on how much time you'd like to invest in marketing and plying your trade. If you decide that you love your new hobby and don't mind spending weekends at craft shows or flea markets or swap meets, then chances are good that your weekdays will be filled replenishing your supply of candles for these events.

Even if you don't think you want to fill your weekends selling, consider the considerable trade the internet carries. A web site, some careful planning and even more careful wrapping and shipping of your product, could net you a substantial part time income.

And then perhaps you'd just like to sell to friends and family on the holidays for special events. You may decide to limit your business to word of mouth trade and even perhaps special orders.

Your success in candle making is limited only by your own desires and imagination.

Eight Quick Tips On
Marketing Your Business

You've set your shingle out -- so to speak -- Candle-maker. And now you sit back in your living room, reading the daily newspaper waiting for the traffic to beat a path to your door.

Uhm? I'm not sure how to tell you this, but as popular as the use of candles is, this is not the ultimate marketing plan. But, there are several steps you can take to help you market your wares. Below are just eight quick ways to get your beautiful candles to the public. And that's the first step in any marketing plan!

1. Create a signature or trademark candle design.

Specialize. Take one candle -- one that you're especially talented at creating -- and make it synonymous with your new, burgeoning business. Is it the gel candle? Are you good at painting on candles? Or perhaps you've got the dipping technique down -- and your customers love it? You may even specialize in beeswax candles.

Decide on a specialty and build your business around this. This doesn't mean you're not going to make other types of candles. Why of course you are! But there's a rule in marketing and the general business world. It's called the 80-20 rule.

This means that 20 percent of your customers make up 80 percent of your profits. Decide what you plan to give your 20 percent of loyal, return customers and you've just established 80 percent of your business.

2. Talk with retailers in your area.

Find out if they are willing to take your candles on consignment. This means you don't get paid unless the retailer sells one of your candles. Of course, with this method of customer acquisition you're not going to break into the Wal-mart market overnight.

But, unless you have a large family and a very wide circle of friends helping you to make those candles by hand, you probably couldn't keep even one Wal-mart store well stocked -- let alone every single one in the nation.

While you're speaking with these retailers, find out if they currently carry any candles and if so, what are their biggest sellers are. You may even be able tailor your candle-making activities towards the sales needs of certain stores in your area.

3. Why rent a store front when you can rent a window?

Sounds weird doesn't it? But it's true! If you want to catch the eye ofhe person who travels the neighborhood -- especially by foot! Is there a vacant office or store front in the town or city you live in. Negotiate with the owner of the building for rental of just the window -- at least until some business moves in.

The advantages to you are tremendous. The rent would be mimimal compared to renting an entire retail space. Plus, on top of that, you get great exposure -- as if you really were renting a storefront.

And even the building owner wins. He brings some

income in from that space even though he hasn't found a retail tenant yet! Sounds like the perfect set up to me!

4. Become the candle-making instructor!

Think about it! What better way to show off your wares . . . display your talents . . . and advertise your business. With a little advertising of the classes themselves and the cooperation of a craft store -- who sells all the candle-making supplies your students will need -- you can start teaching others.

You may even want to hold smaller courses right in your home or rent a church hall that has a stove. If you seriously give this option some thought, you'l come up with lots of varieties on this theme!

After just a class or two, you've set yourself up as the authority on the subject of candle-making and get your name and business in the public's eye!

5. Rent a flea market booth -- or two!

Work during the week, but have weekends free? Why not rent a booth at a local flea market? Rental fees are relatively cheap, especially considering the amount of traffic some of these events bring.

If you're not familiar with your area's flea markets, you definitely want to make the rounds before you decide on which market from which to rent your booth. There are several aspects to consider when you choosing. First, how many --if any -- other entrepreneurs are specializing in candles?

And if there are several, do you think you can successfully compete with them? What makes your product stand head and shoulders above the ones already there?

Don't be hesitant about talking to the vendors already selling at the flea market. Get a feel to see what kind of atmosphere it is, if they consider themselves making any kind of money and if the traffic that's currently at the market is normal. Do many people come, but few buy?

Take all this information -- and anything else you can think to ask -- into account when making your decision.

Many flea markets run only on weekends. Others run not only on weekends, but one day during the week -- in some regions of the country this third day is Wednesday.

If your first choice of a rental booth is at a market that only opens Saturday and Sunday, why not check out another flea market where you can reach a steady customer base on a third day as well?

In this way, you can at least catch some of the traffic in this second location. Or you may want to enlist the aid of family members and close friends. If one of them agrees to staff a booth, you could offer them a percentage of the sales!

6. Create a small catalog

Why not? With a decent digital camera, the photos of your candles will probably sell themselves. And, at least at first, your distribution area doesn't need to be tremendously large. You can hand these out just about to everyone. In fact, when you get a booth at the flea market you can set a stack on your table.

You can even give these out to students at your

candle-making classes. And whenever you sell a candle, give your customer a catalog.

And printing costs can be kept to a minimum at first as well. If you have a color printer then you can print just a few at a time -- only what you think you'll need.

7. Market yourself as a "custom" candle maker.

That's right! Tell your potential customers that -- unlike many craftsmen or especially craft stores, you'd be glad to take specific orders. This may especially be popular during the holidays.

8. Give away free samples.

No, I'm not talking about passing out your most expensive and most beautiful creations. What I am talking about is taking advantage of today's popularity of the tealights.

Create tealights in your most popular scents and colors. Pass these out to interested individuals, whether it be at flea markets or craft shows, or just to those who stop to talk.

In fact, you could include a free tealight candle with every purchase a customer makes, just to provide him with an idea of your wide range of talents -- and merchandise. And your customer will appreciate the gift. Chances are she'll be back -- and bring a friend.

Don't quite know which direction to head in your business? This statistic might give you a good idea. Industry research shows the most influential factor in candle purchases is the scent. Far behind this consideration are color and shape. Scent it and they will come!

Believe it or not, now is a renaissance period for candle purchases. Overall, the sales of candles are growing faster than the economy as a whole. Your business is looking more encouraging by the minute, now isn't it?

So now you've just about talked yourself into testing the waters for your candle business. But you now have to decide what type of candles to make. Would it help if you knew where your potential customers were going to use your products? Of course. Yes, I have numbers on that too.

Candles by the numbers

When you know what rooms of the house your customers plan on burning these in, you can create candles that blend in with appropriate decorations and designs. For example, 42 percent of the individuals survey said they burn their candles primarily in their living room. About 18 percent use candles in the kitchen and only 13 percent use them in a bedroom.

Not only that, but I even know who buys these candles. Your potential market is made up first and foremost of women. In fact, more than 96 percent of all candles are bought by women. Females also use candles more often than men and younger people use candles more often than older folks.

There you have it. Thinking twice about entering the business now? You've got an idea of who you're selling to -- and you've got some sound marketing tips. You've probably already have some type of "inventory" lying around. You know you're making candles faster than you and your friends combined can burn them.

Hey! Where are you going? Oh, you're out to check out flea markets. Oh . . . so you are ready to stake out a candle-company territory.

I'll keep a candle burning for you!

Conclusion

This, unfortunately, is the end of the book, but I suspect it's only the beginning of a long and happy relationship with candle making. At the very least, I have a feeling you'll continue to supply all your house hold needs with your own quality creations.

And no doubt you should. But I'm also betting that you're already sharing some of your better samples with friends and family. And you've probably already decided what type of candle Aunt Mary Ann is getting for Christmas and how you're going to make Cousin Jane's candle different from your friend's JoAnne's candle.

Oh yes. You've got the candle making "bug." It's not a bad vice to be saddled with -- and speak from experience.

As you continue on your journey, I know that your creativity will grow along with your skill as a candle maker. But more than that, as I mentioned earlier in this book, you're creating the most important thing of all: memories.

If you make candles with your children, these will be the days they recall fondly. And they may even decide to pass the tradition on to their children.

You're making memories with family members. Every time you give a candle you've made by hand, you've given a portion of yourself.

You're making memories with friends. As they accept, display and use your gift of creativity, they'll be reminded of all the great times you've spent together.

Keep the candles burning!

Appendix
Essential Tools of Candle Making

Essential tool	Used to . . . .
Candle dye chips	dye melted wax
Candle Molds	Contain and conform shape of candles
Candle Scents	Provide fragrances
Candle Thermometer	Gauge temperature of melting wax
Containers	contain soft waxes while burning.
Craft scissors	trim soft candle wax and wicks.
Double Boiler	melt candle wax
Hammer and screwdriver	to break apart large chunks of wax
Heating element	To melt wax (stove or hot plate)
Kitchen or postal scale	To weigh ingredients on special projects
Large plastic trash bag	prevent scattering chips while breaking wax
Measuring cups	measure liquid ingredients
Measuring spoons	mix dyes and scents into melted wax. Use separate spoons for each dye color.
Mold release	coat inside of molds for easy candle removal
Mold sealer	secure wick and seal wick holes

	in molds
Paper towels	help with general clean up as you make the candles and when you've completed each project.
Paring Knife	cut soft cold wax and trim candles
Pencils	hold wicks in place while creating candles
Primed wicks	burn candles; have been chemically treated
Tape measure	Measure candles and wick dimensions

REFERENCES

Web Sites

http://www.peakcandle.com/category/Wicks.aspx, accessed 03 Jun 09

http://candleandsoap.about.com/od/canclemakingbasics/a/candlebasics.htm , accessed 03 Jun 09

Making pillar candles, http://www.peakcandle.com/pillarcandlemaking.aspx, accessed 7 Jun 09

Making hand-dipped candles,
http://www.pioneerthinking.com/dipped.html,
accessed 8 Jun 09

How do I melt gel wax?,
http://candleandsoap.about.com/od/gelcandlemakin
gfaqs/f/FAQGelwaxmelt.htm, accessed 8 Jun 09

How to make gel candles,
http://www.ehow.com/how_18059_make-gel-
candles.html, accessed 8 Jun 09

**7 Tips To Market Your Candle Making Business For
Maximum Profit,** http://teenmoneymakingideas.com/7-
tips-to-market-your-candle-making-business-for-
maximum-profit/, access 9 Jun 09

How to make hand-dipped candles,
http://www.pioneerthinking.com/dipped.html ,
accessed 10 Jun 09

How to make gel candles,
http://www.pioneerthinking.com/tt_gelcandles.html,
accessed 10 Jun 09

Making votive candles,
http://www.pioneerthinking.com/tt_gelcandles.html,
accessed 8 Jun 09

Making Soy Candles,
http://candles.lovetoknow.com/Making_Soy_Candles ,
accessed 10 Jun 09

Books

Abadie, Marie-Jeannie, **The Everything Candle making
Book,** Adams Media,2002, Cincinnati, Ohio, accessed

through Google books, 03 Jun 09.

Vanessa-Ann, ***Candle making for the First Time,*** Sterling Publishing Co., Inc., New York City, NY, 2001

2131201R00061

Printed in Great Britain
by Amazon.co.uk, Ltd.,
Marston Gate.